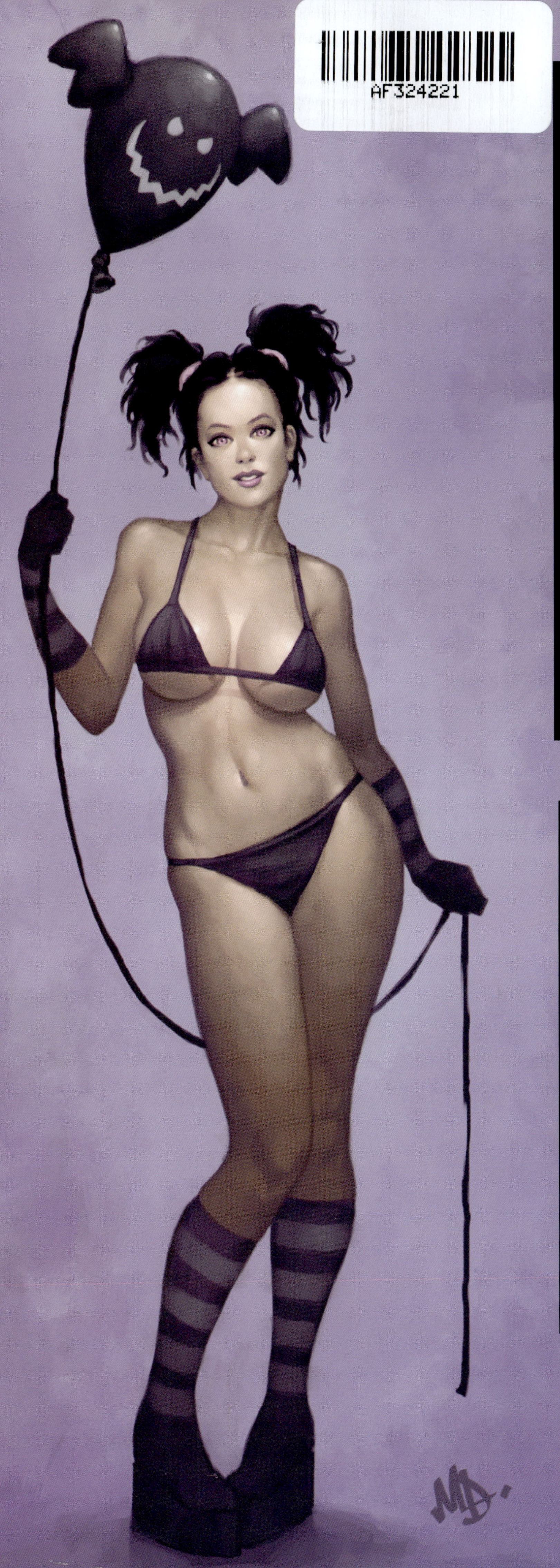

GIRLS ON TOP!

the pin-up art of MATT DIXON

AN SQP PRESENTATION

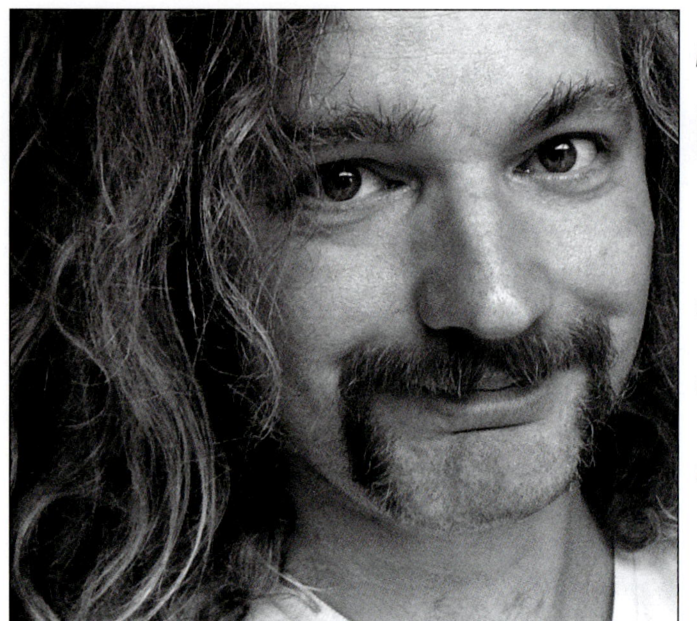

MATT DIXON:
"A bad attitude is a thing of beauty!"

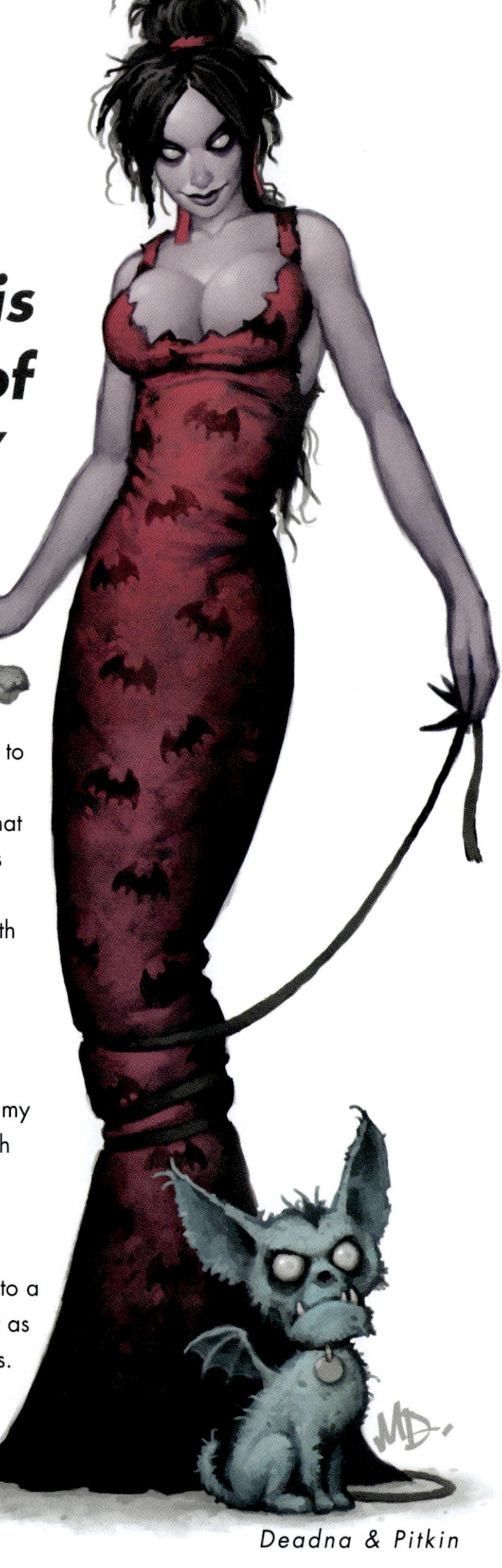

"A friend once told me that the girl in the pinup painting I'd just shown to her looked, 'like she's about to kick someone's ass all over town'.

I've yet to receive a higher compliment.

I don't want to see a girl draped helplessly at the feet of a bare-chested barbarian or lashed to a tree outside a dragon's lair while she waits patiently for the arrival of a knight in shining armor. Those chicks don't interest me. I want to see the kind of girl who'd roundhouse kick that barbarian dude in his werewolf pelt jockeys, take his sword along with any gold coins in his possession, then set out to do battle with the kingdom's most ferocious dragon and rescue her captive chum, before they both wind up in some nearby tavern to end the day with a girly chat over a few well earned mugs of chilled ale and a platter full of unicorn burgers.

Perhaps my girls don't look all that different from those defenseless fantasy babes. I've certainly drawn my fair share of tin bikinis and breasts that miraculously remain contained despite being restrained by no more than a scrap of fur and a prayer, but the difference isn't in costume or the curves, it's in the attitude. Attitude is something I try to give my pinup girls plenty of. Generous scoops of hell raising, fun loving, ass kicking, lip curling, high volume heavy metal attitude. With rainbow sprinkles and plenty of chocolate sauce.

Painting these girls has been a lot of fun. I hope they're fun to look at too."

Matt Dixon is an illustrator and concept artist based in the UK. Contributing his first art to a videogame in 1988 at the tender age of 16 led to a long career in the games industry, first as a production artist, then as an art lead on numerous high profile titles. Now freelance, Matt continues to work with clients in the videogame industry in addition to print and online media. His favorite color is green. Matt can be contacted through his website – **www.mattdixon.co.uk**

Deadna & Pitkin

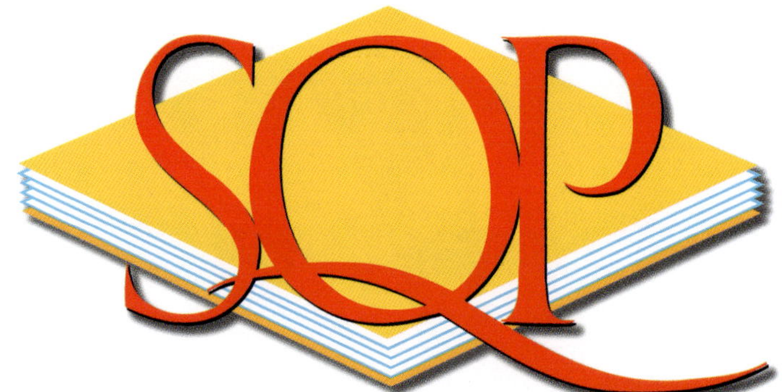

For a free full color catalog showcasing the entire SQP line of erotic, fantasy, and pin-up artwork, go to:

www.sqpartbooks.com

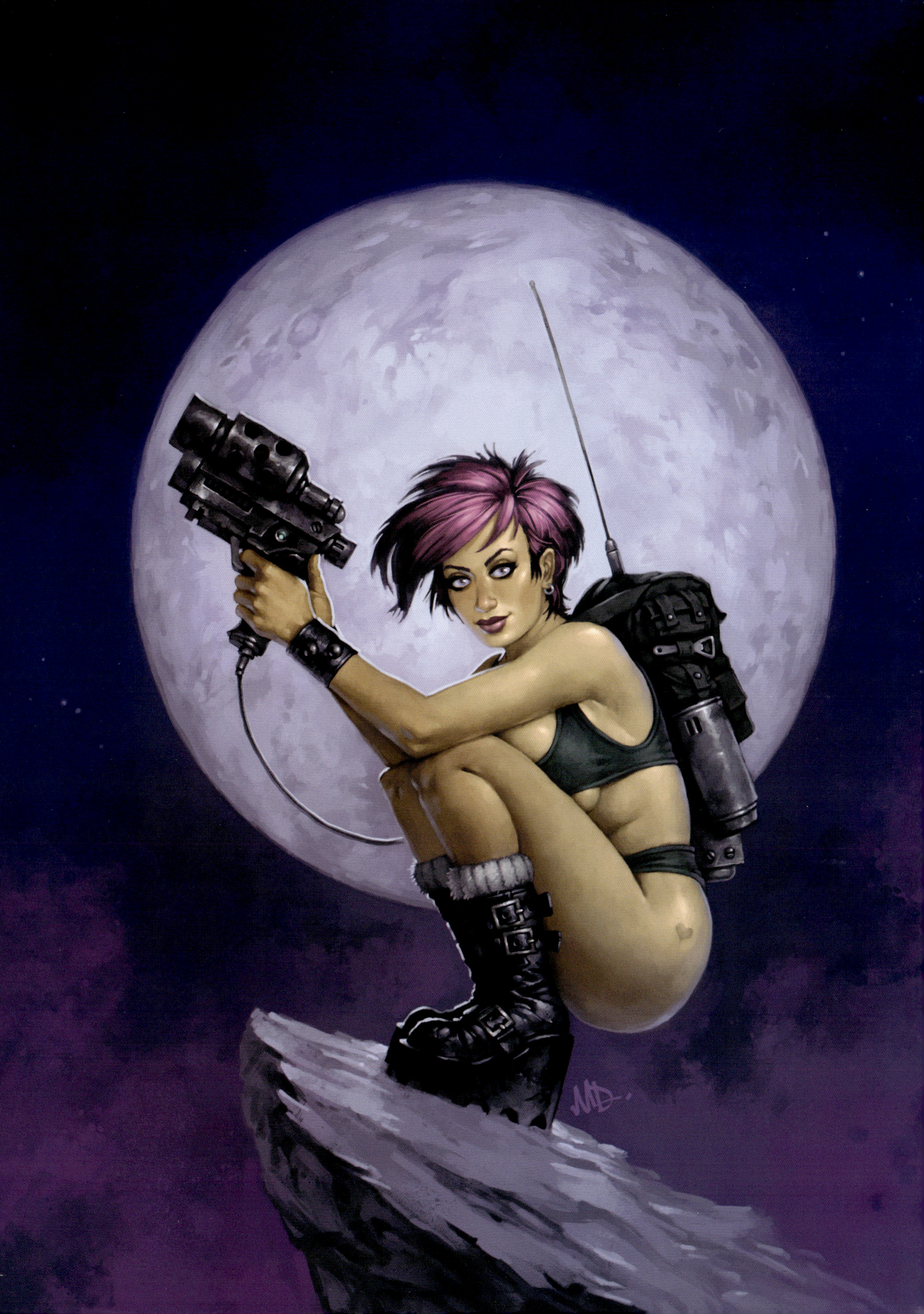

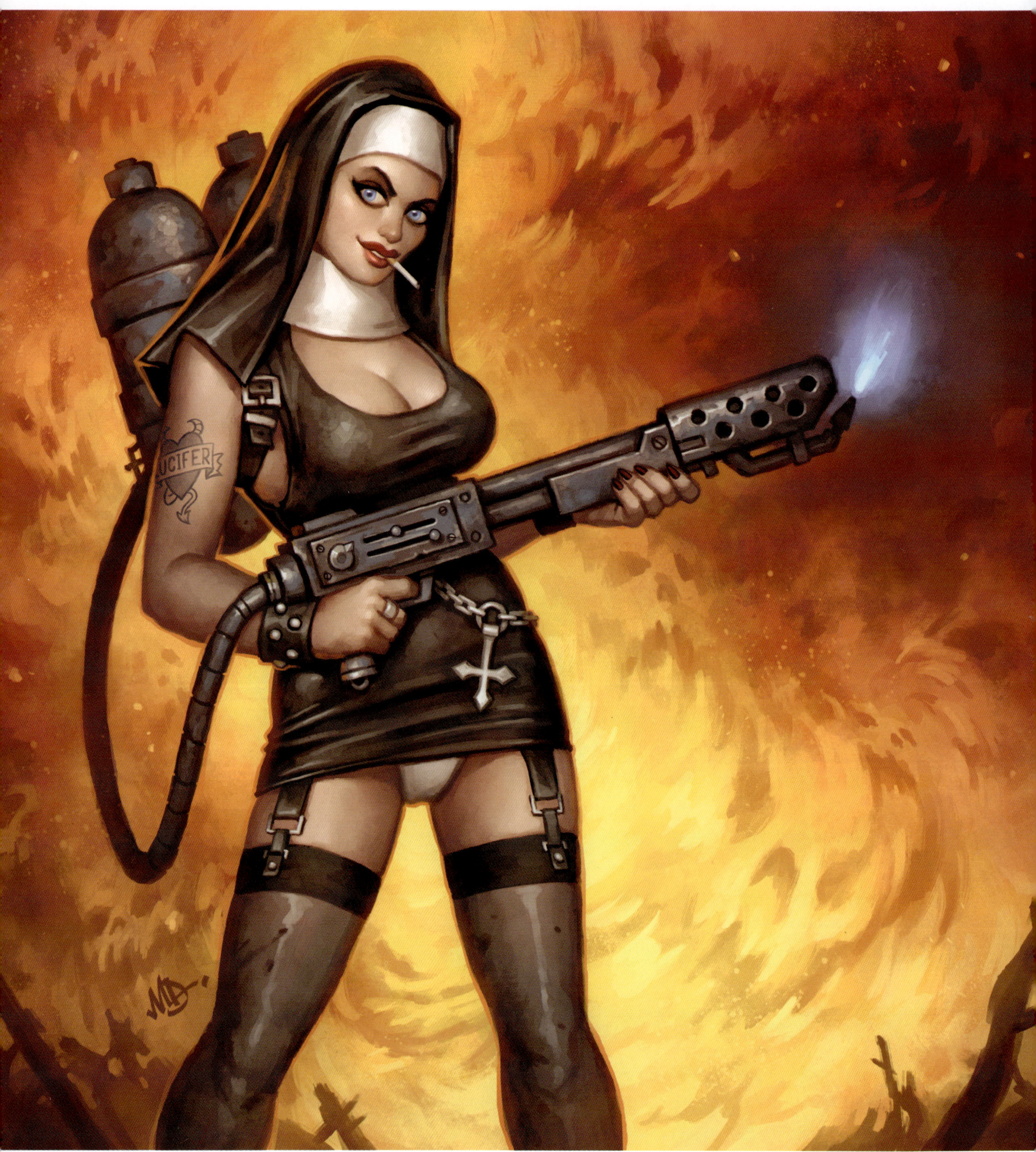

Second To Nun

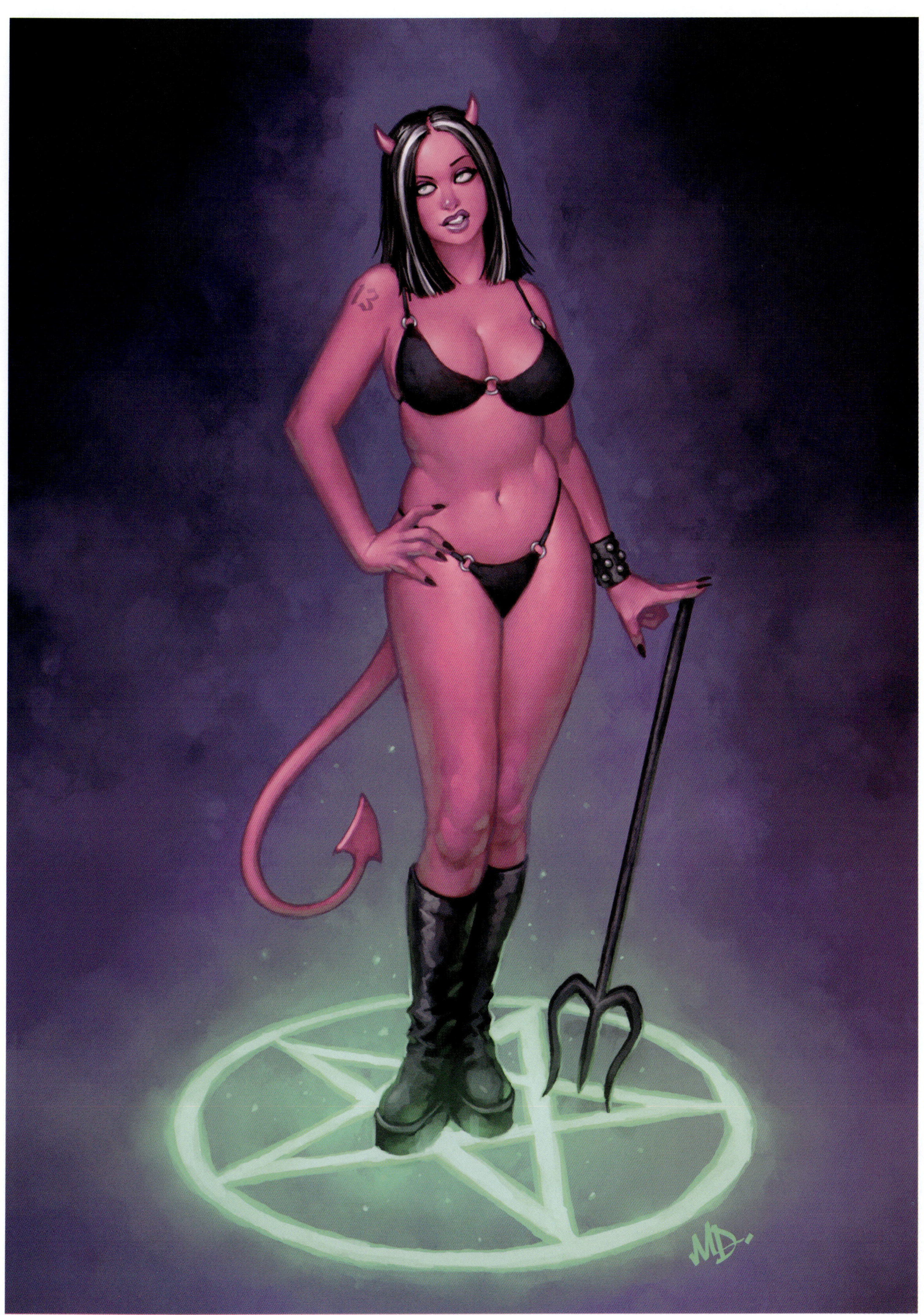

Lucyfer

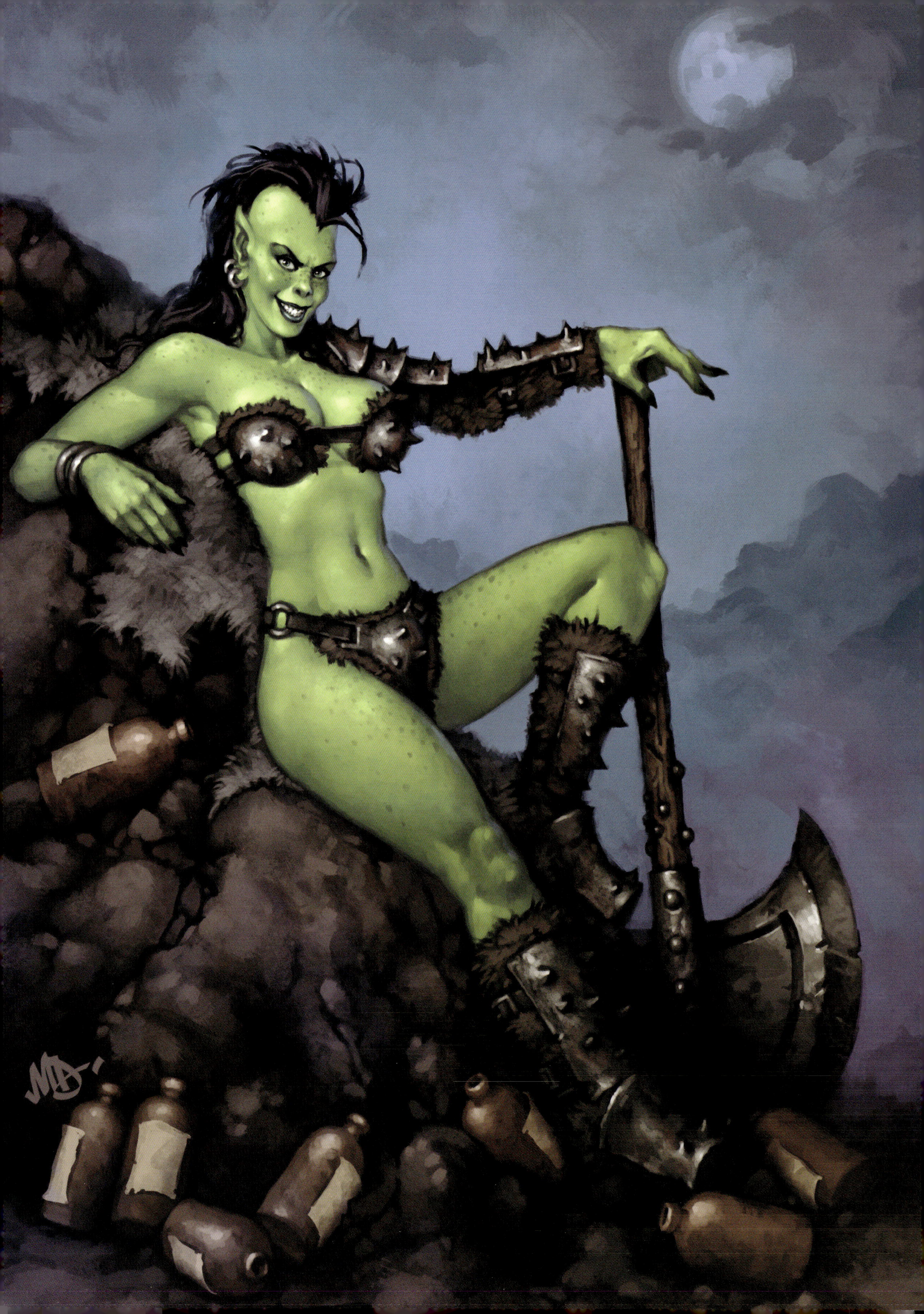

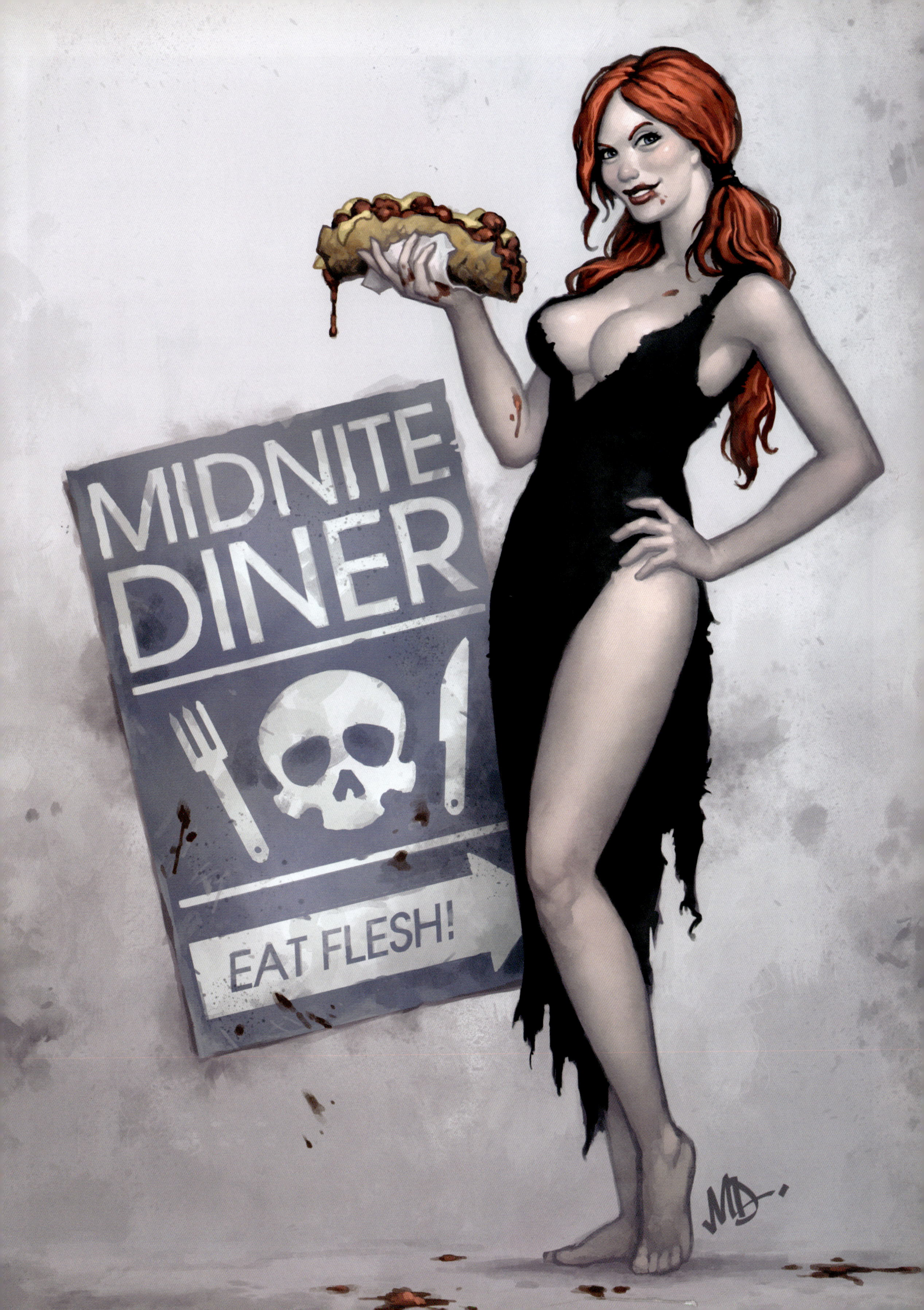
MIDNITE
DINER
EAT FLESH!

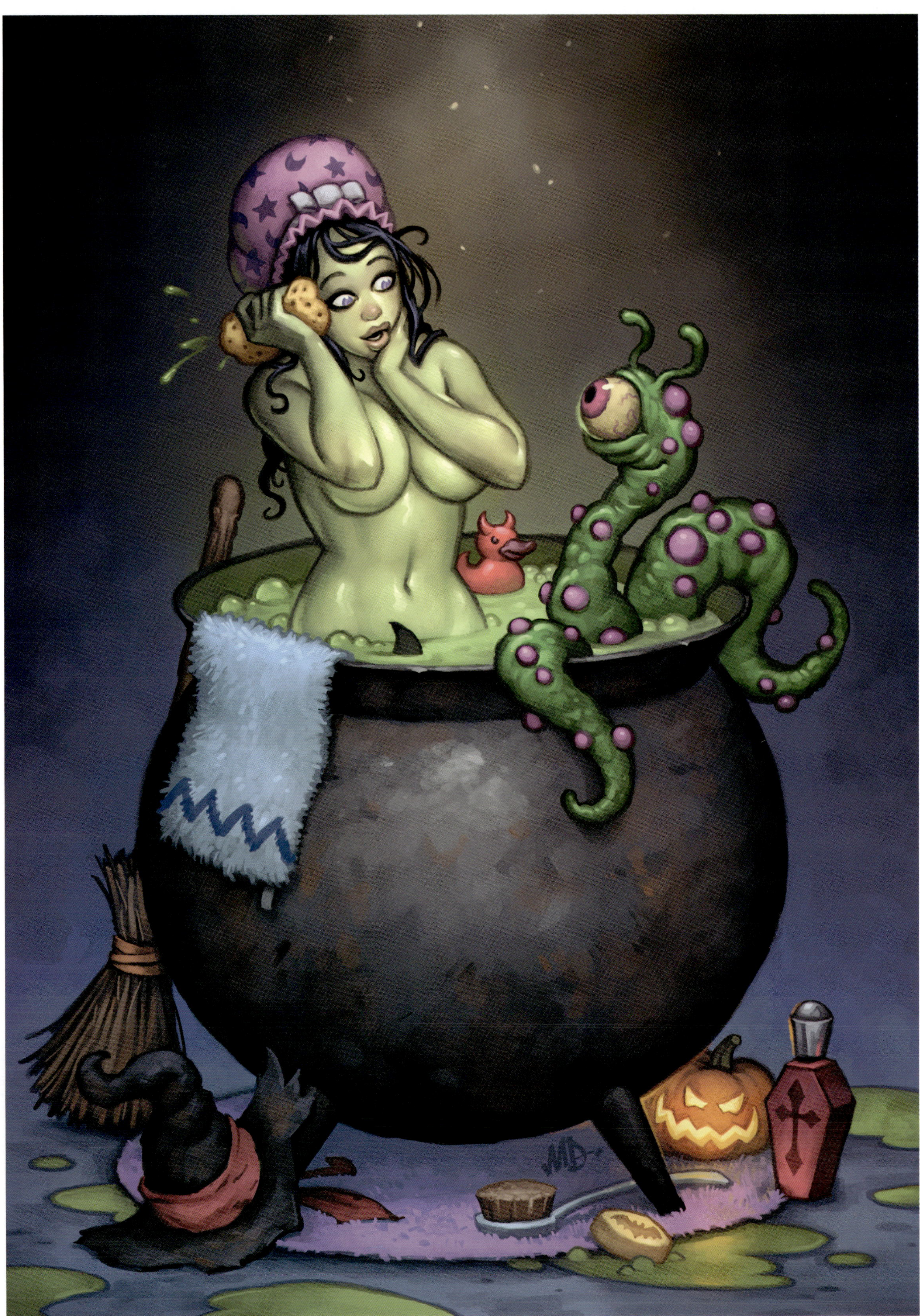

Bathtime

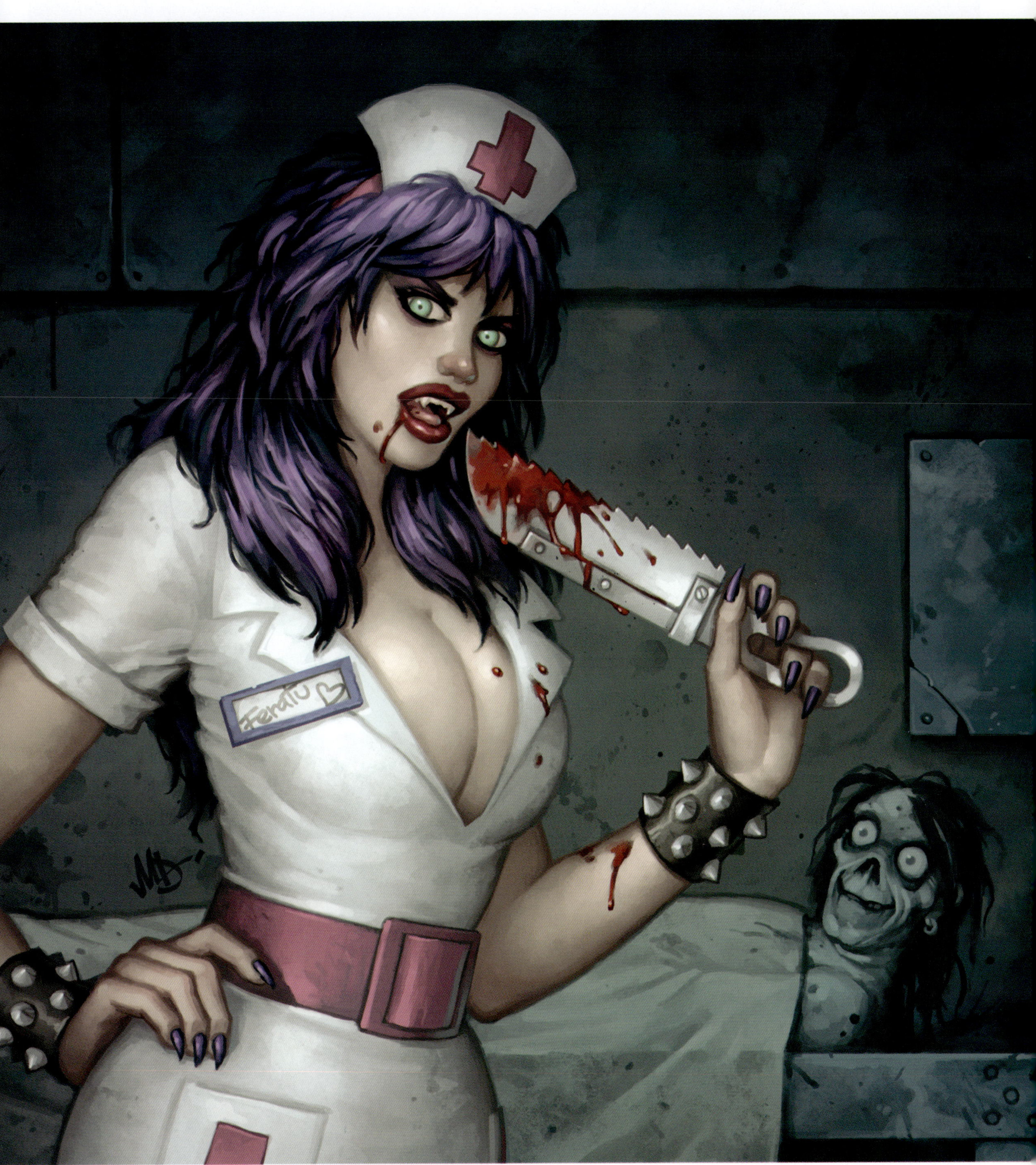

Nurse Feratu

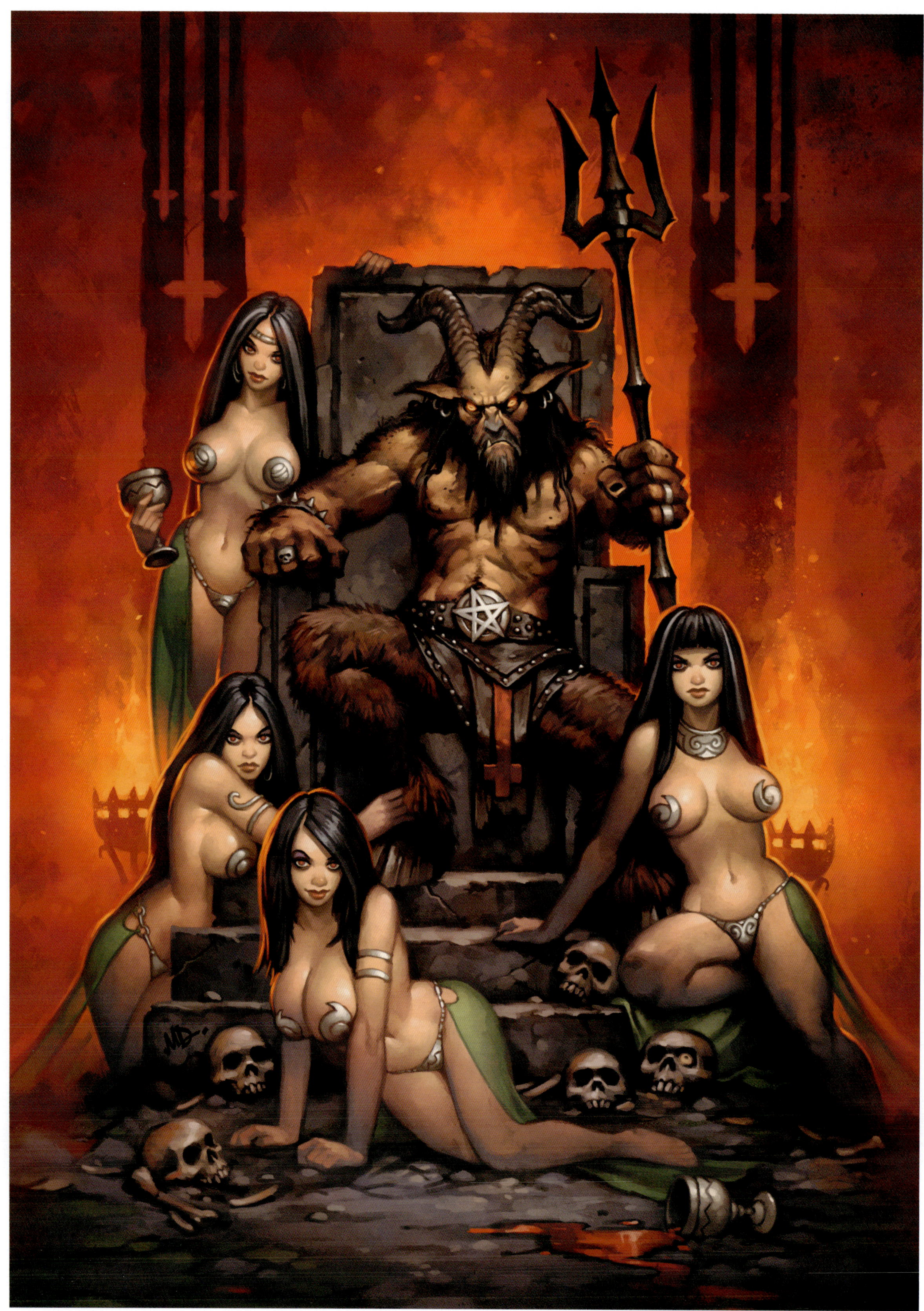

Hells Belles

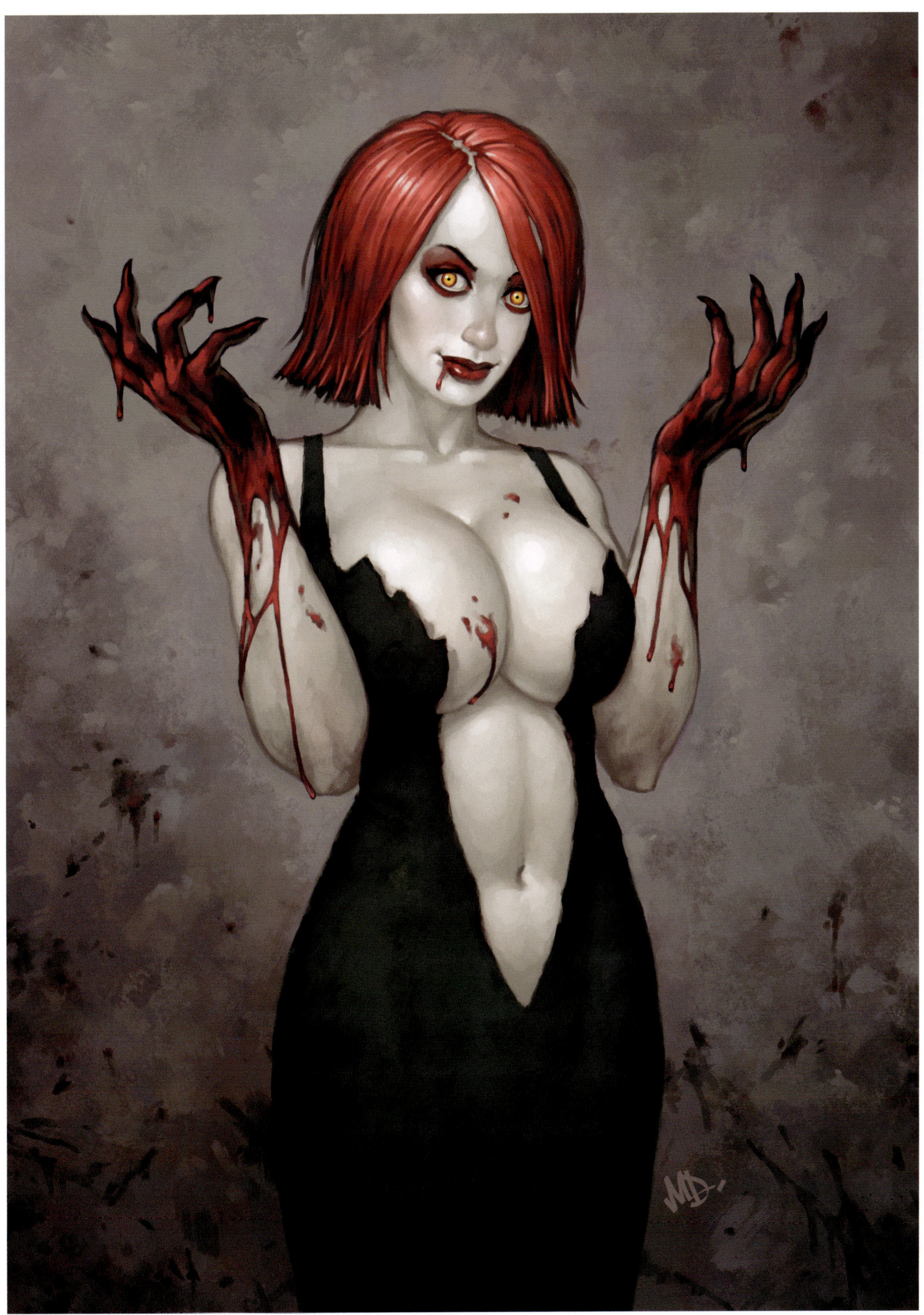

Type "OH!"

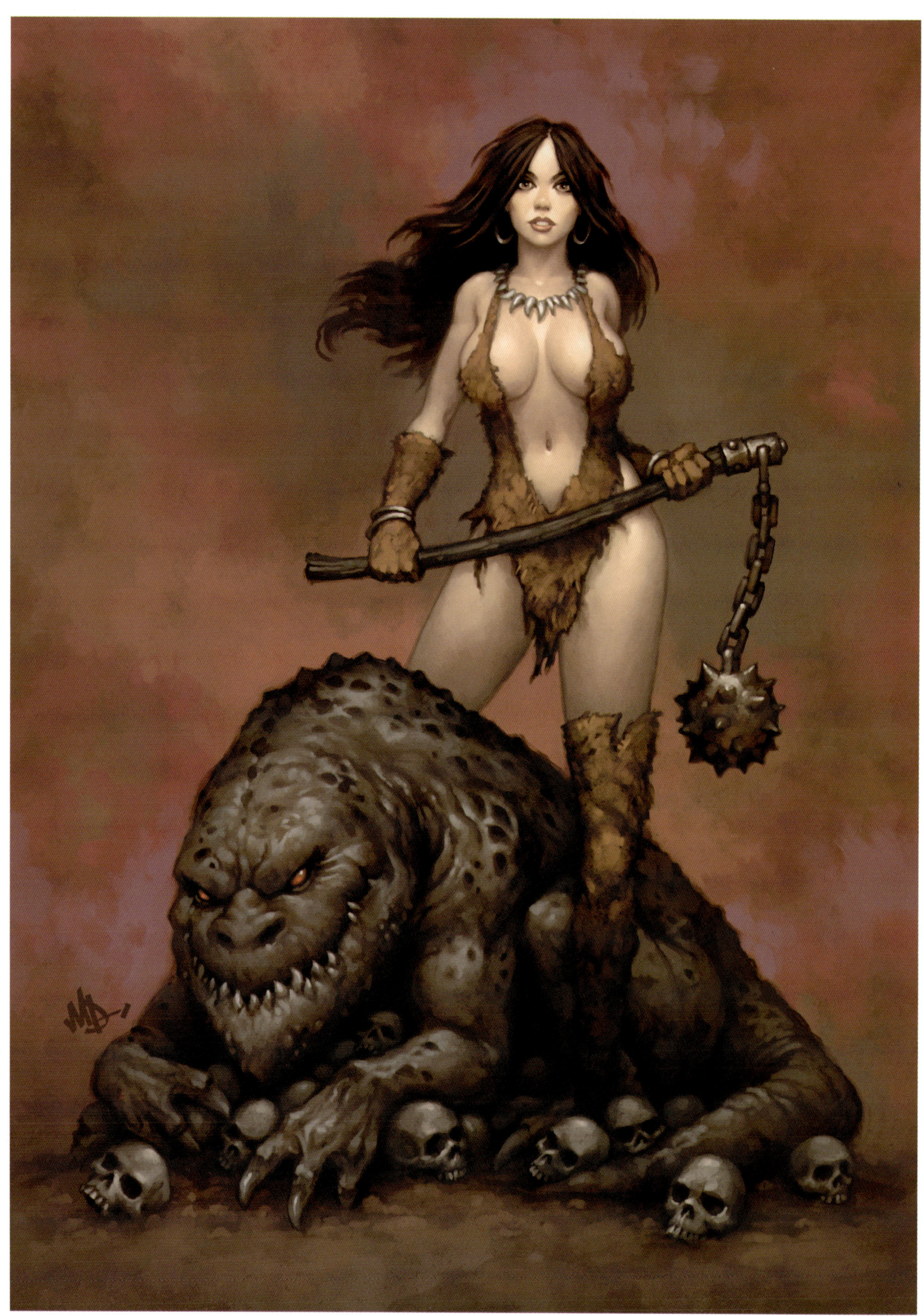

Bambi & Thumper

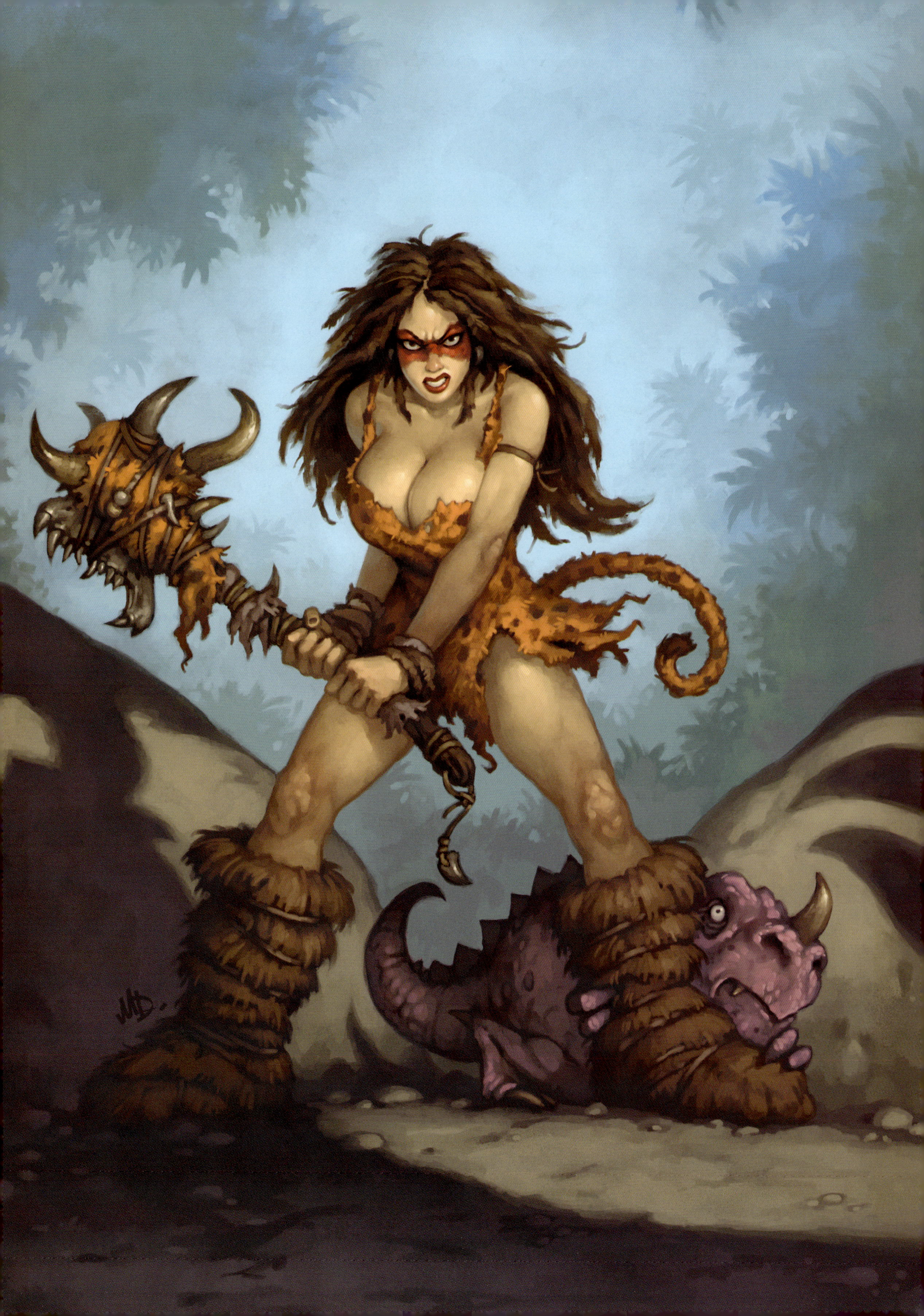

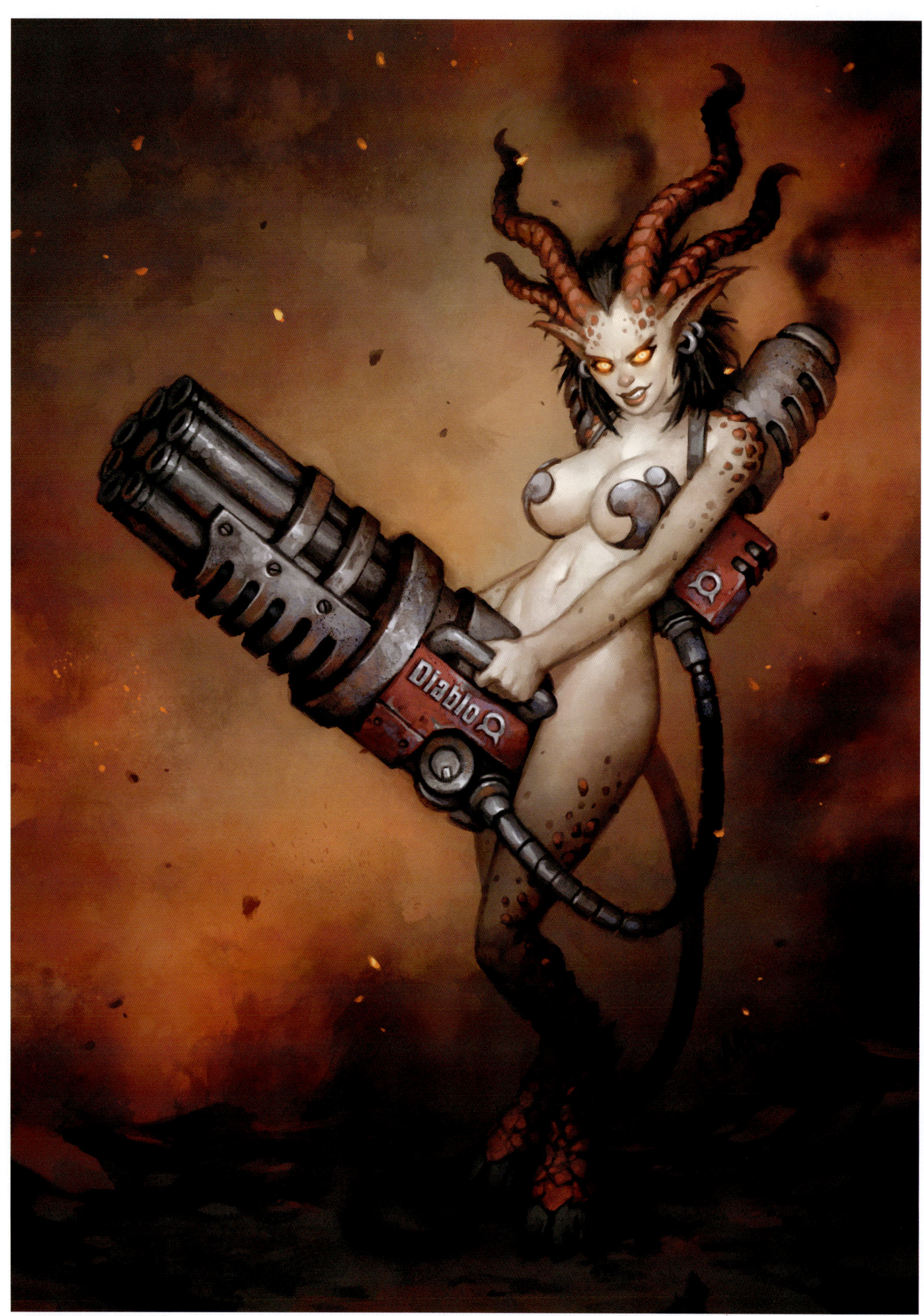

Diesel Driven Damsel of Doom

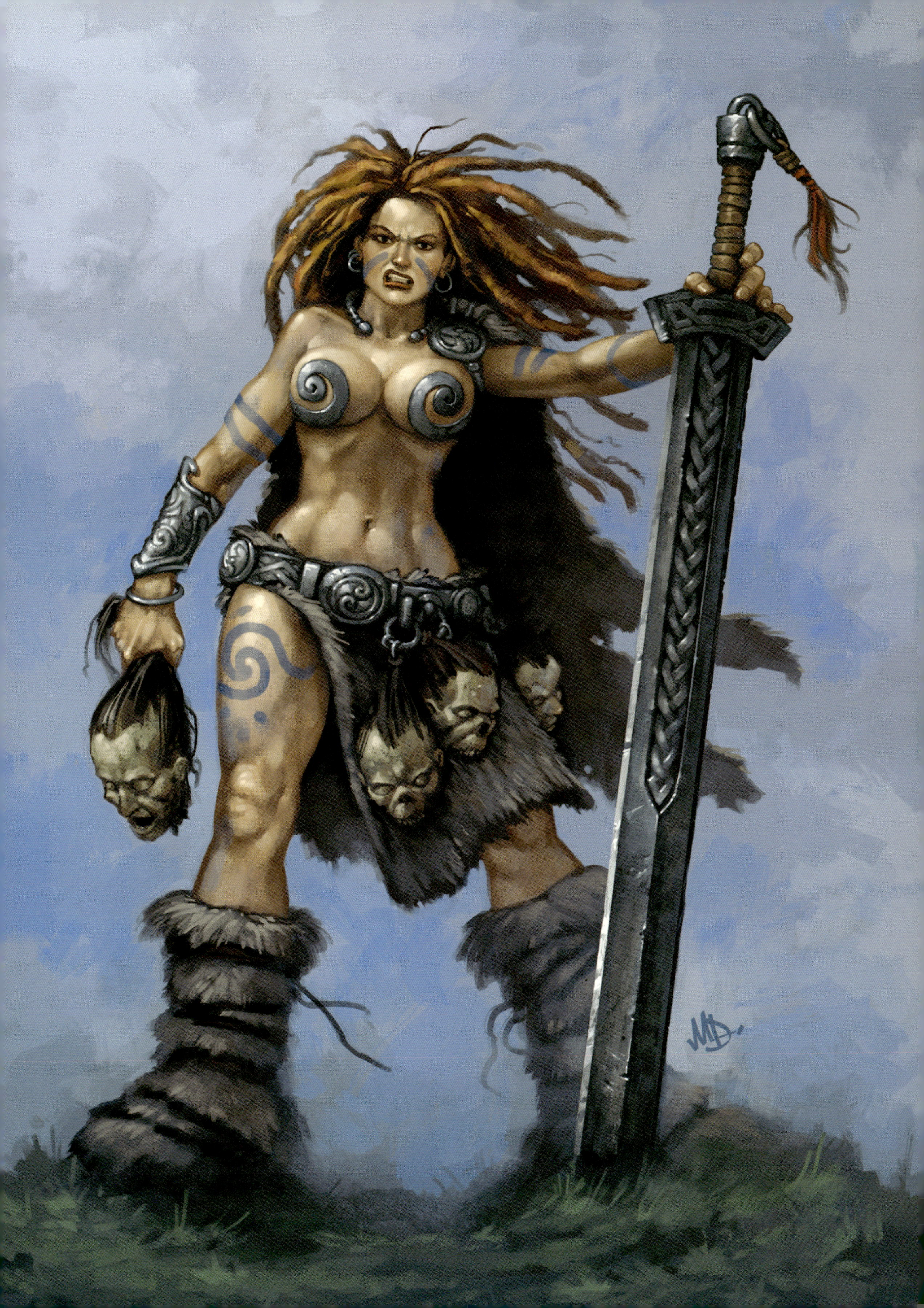

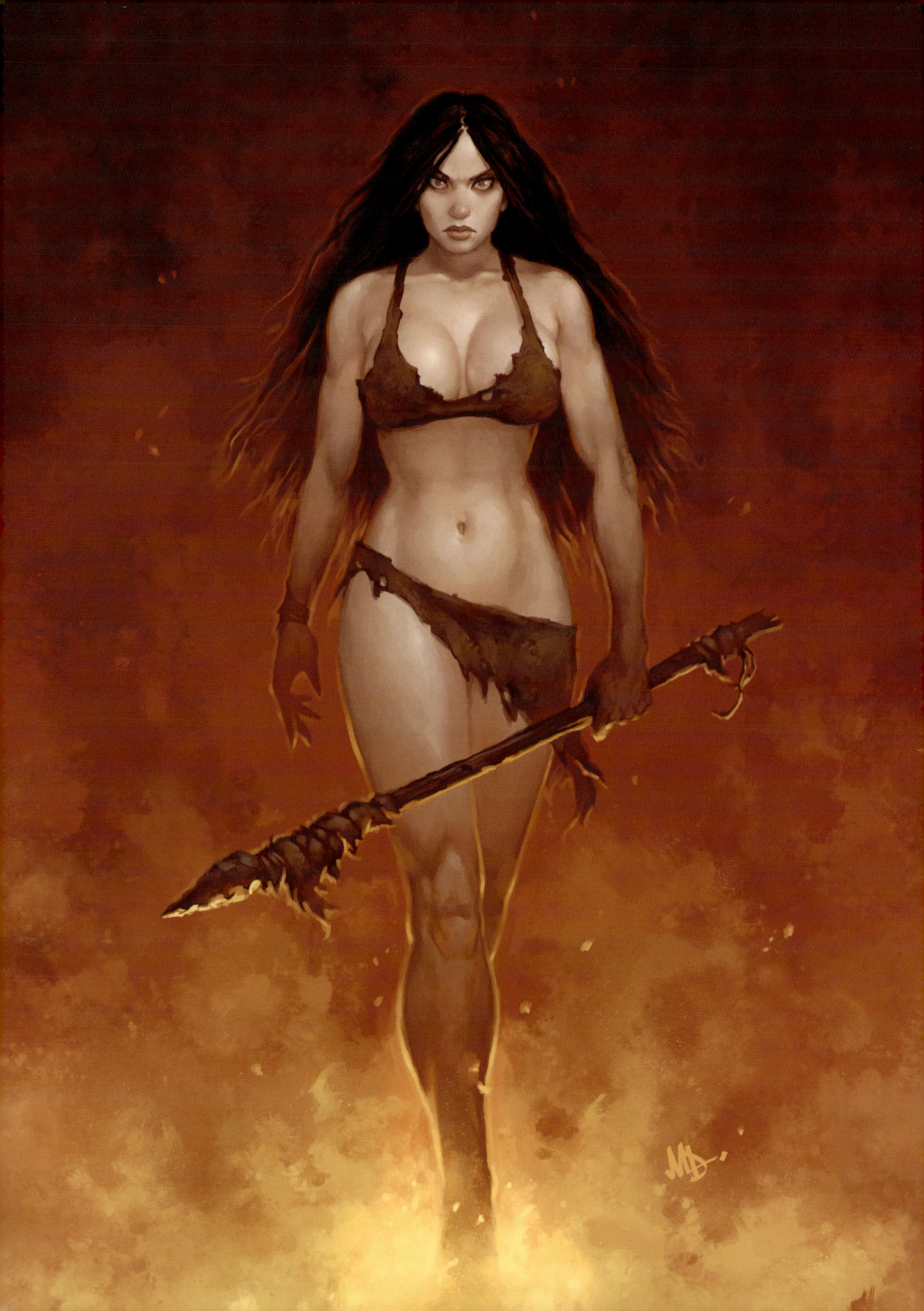

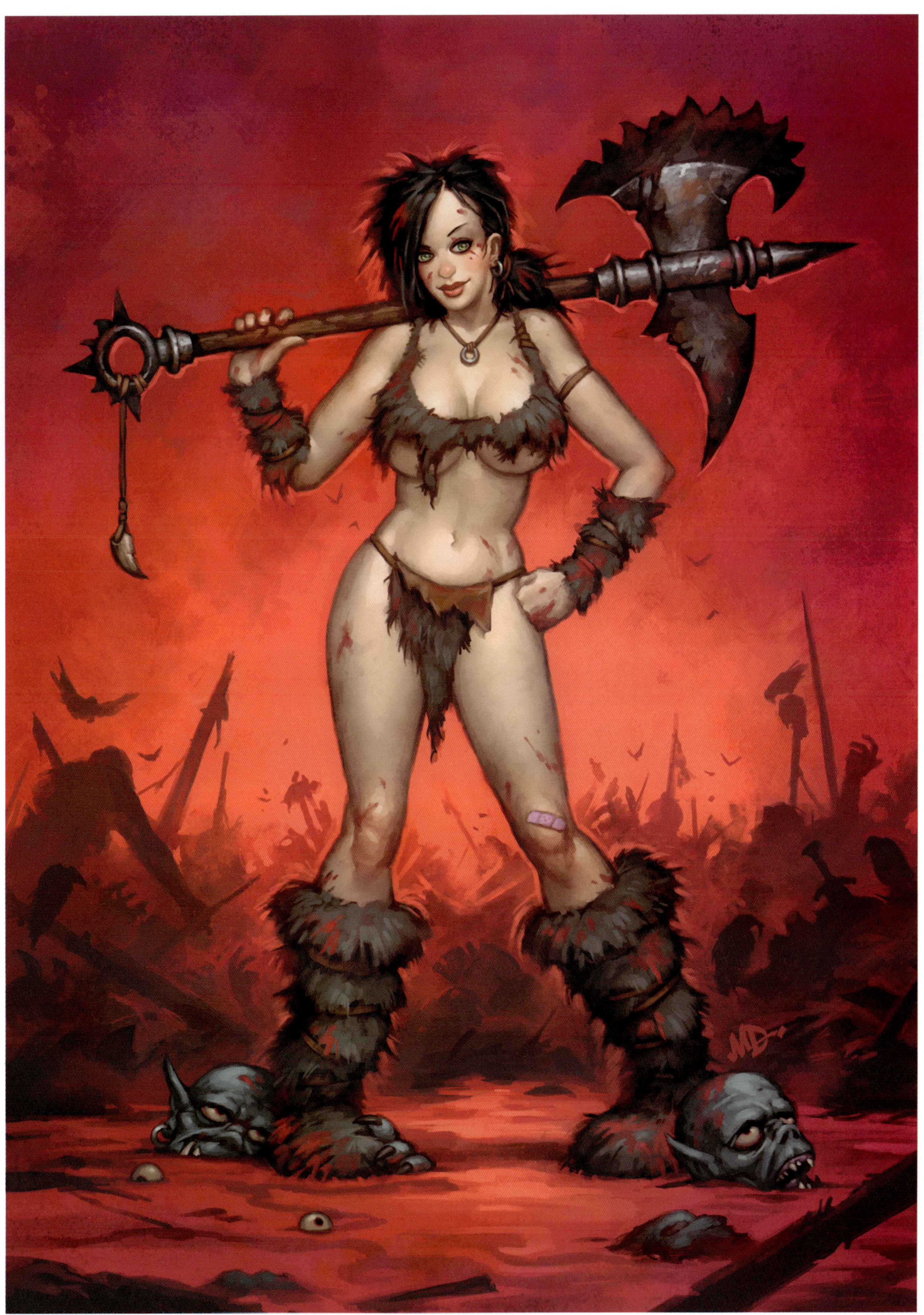

Barbarianne

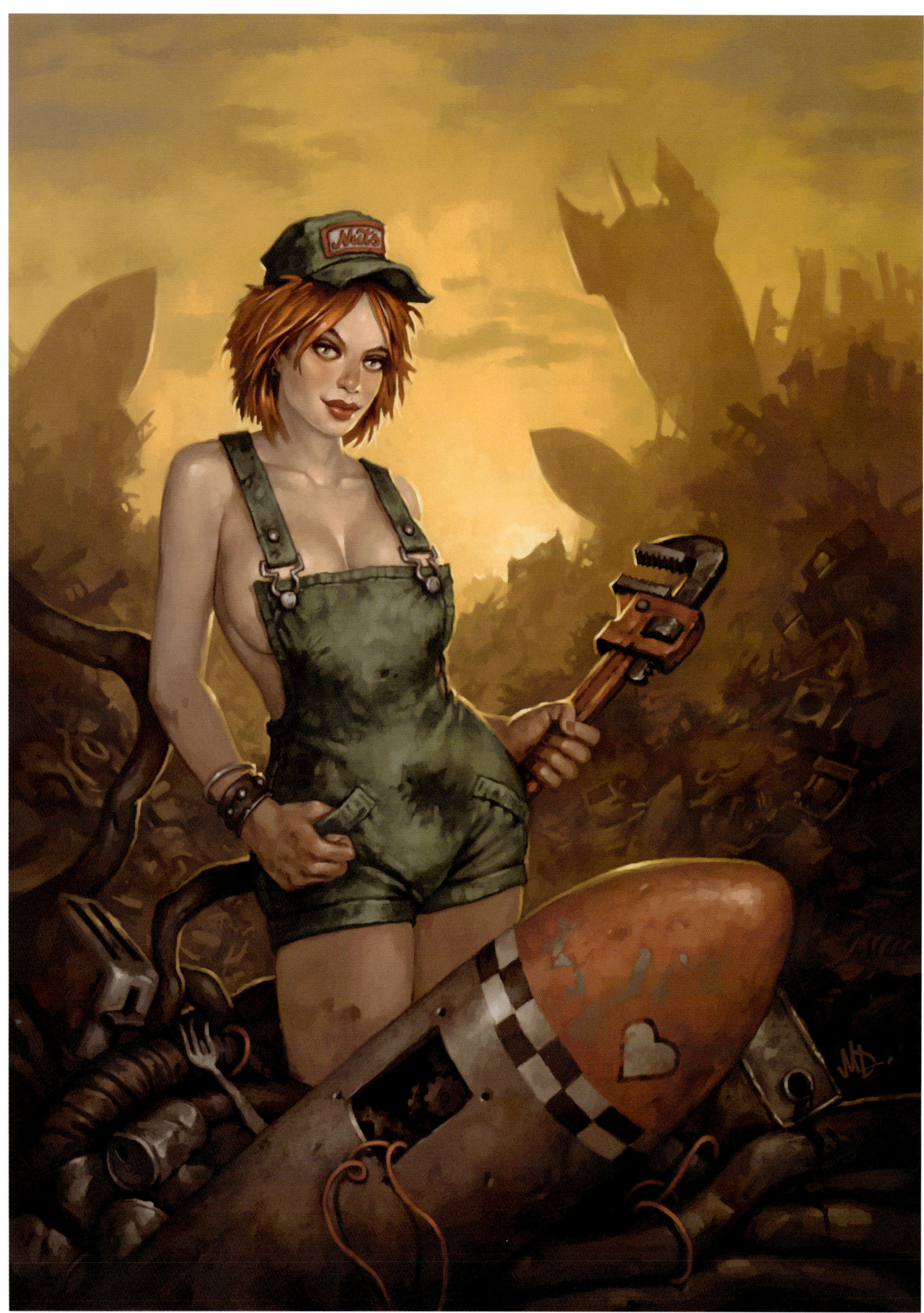

Rocket Science

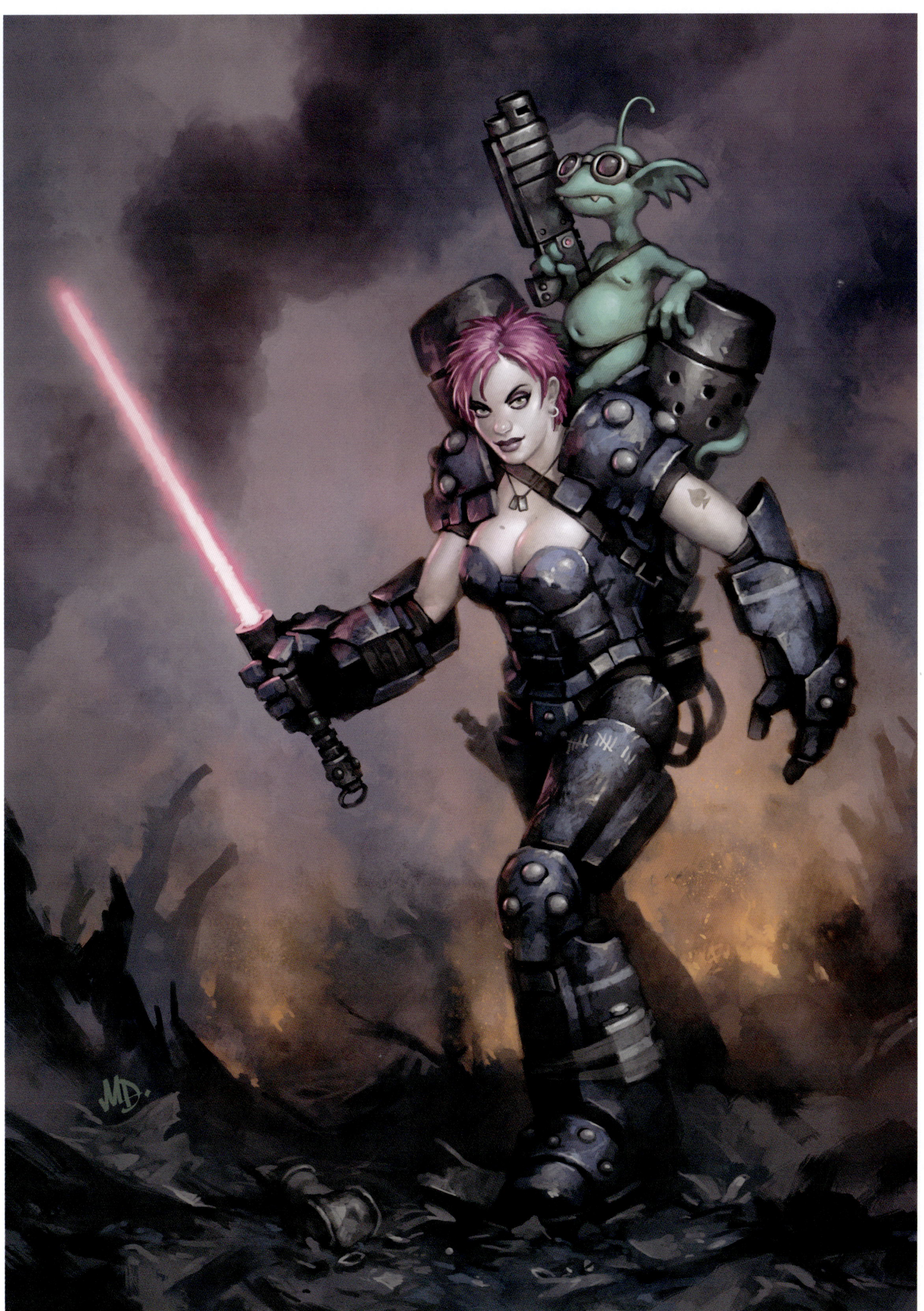

Pop 'n' Chop

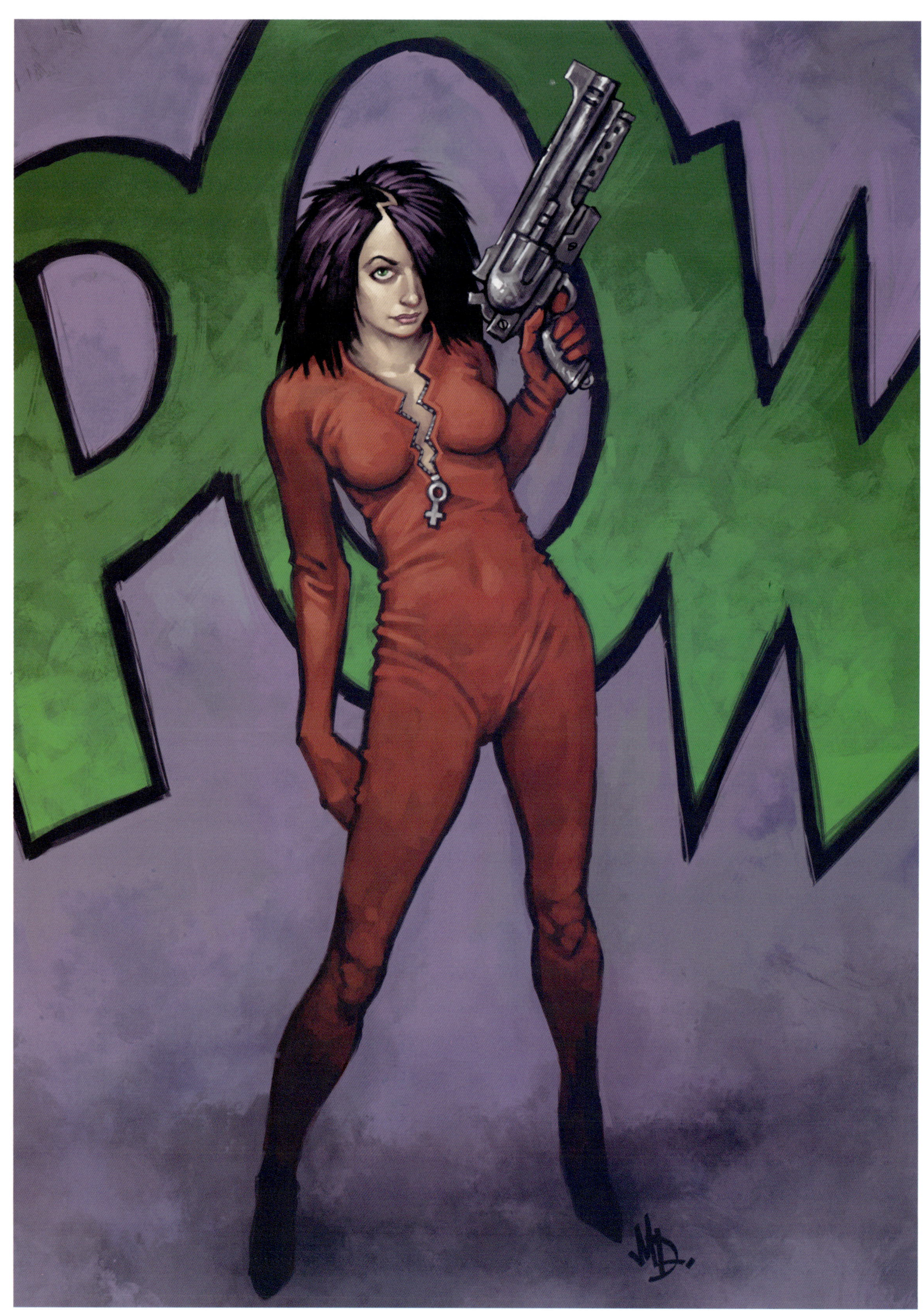

Anna Matopeia

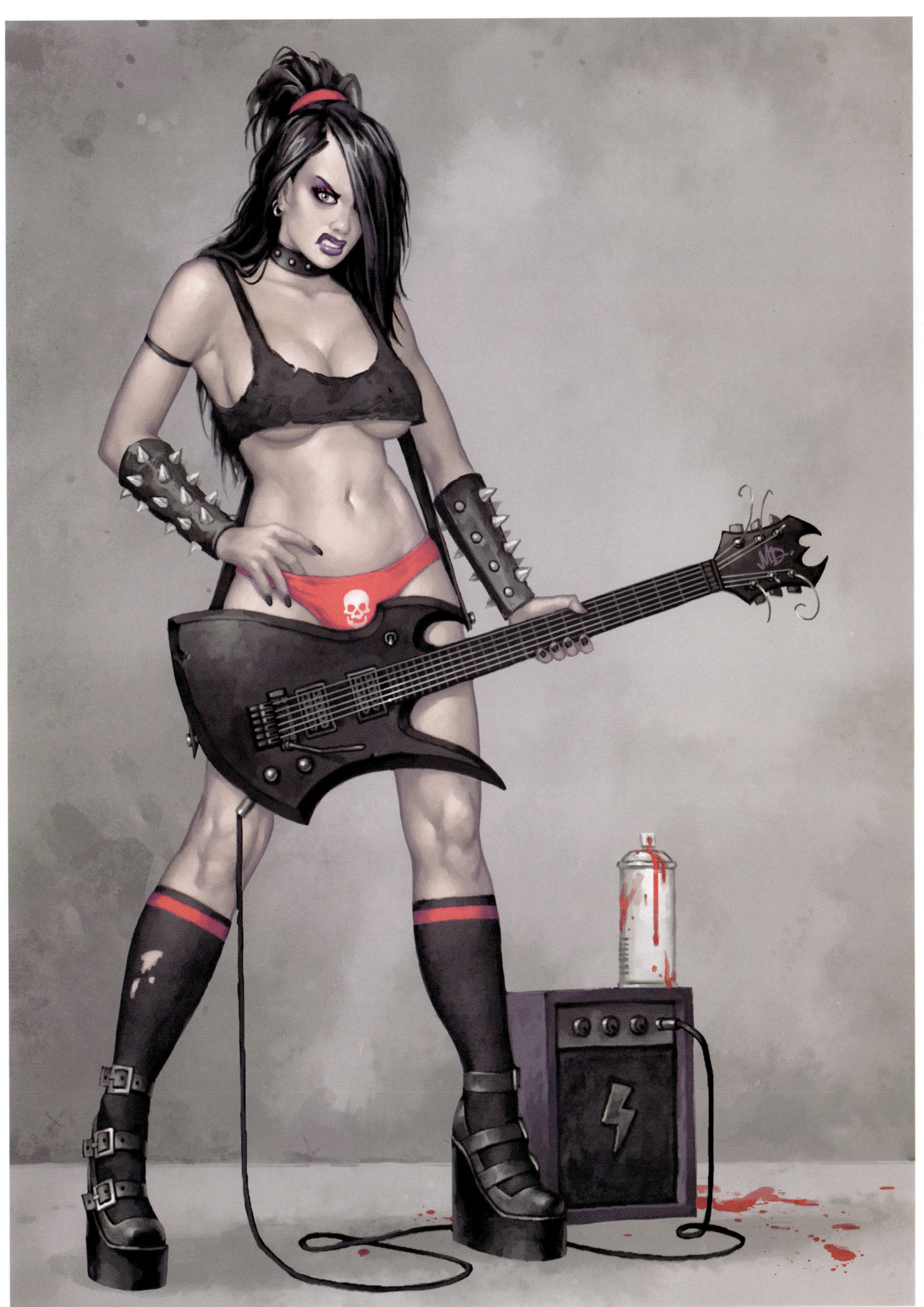

Death Metal Darlin'

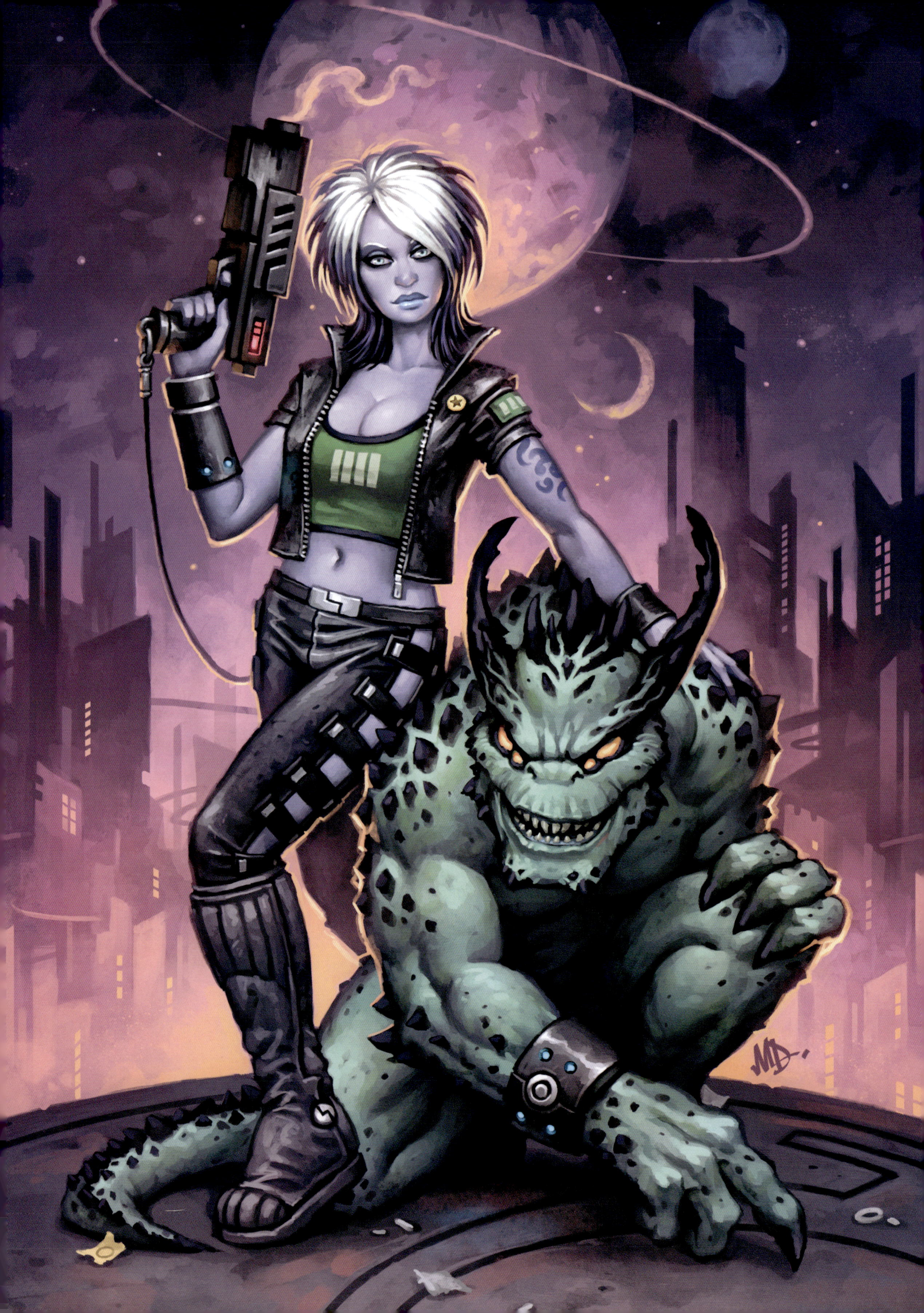

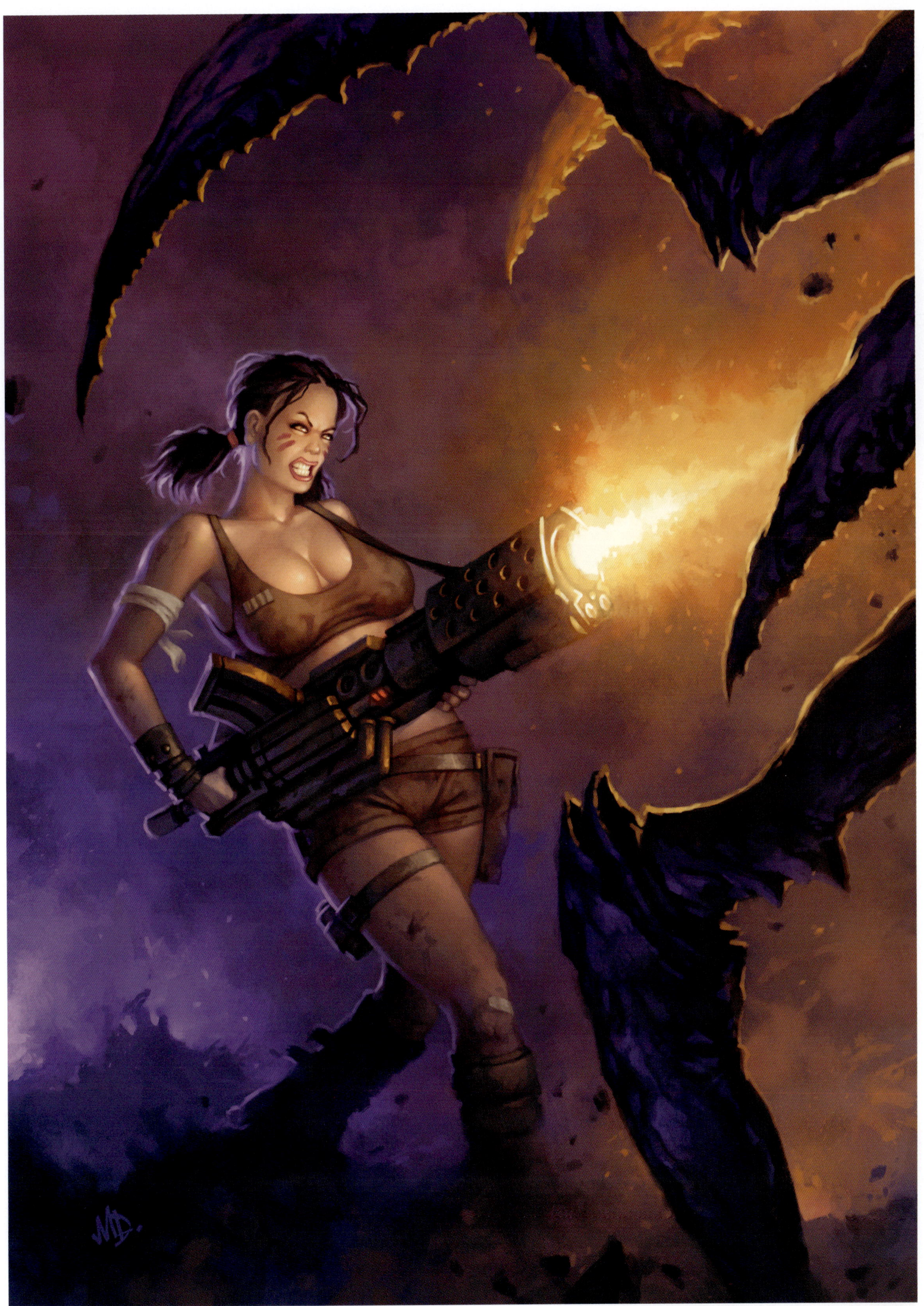

Bug Spray

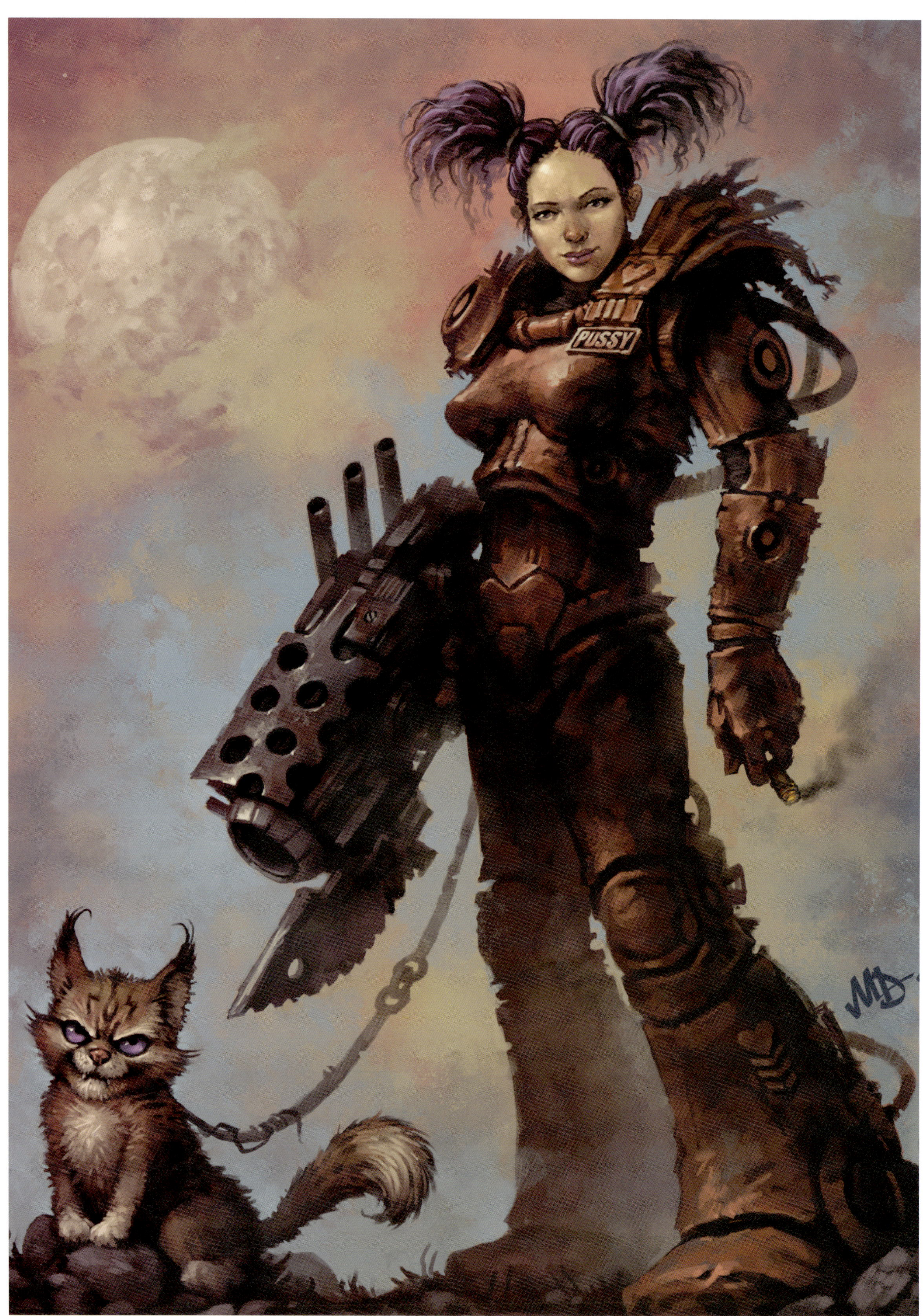

Pussy Patrol

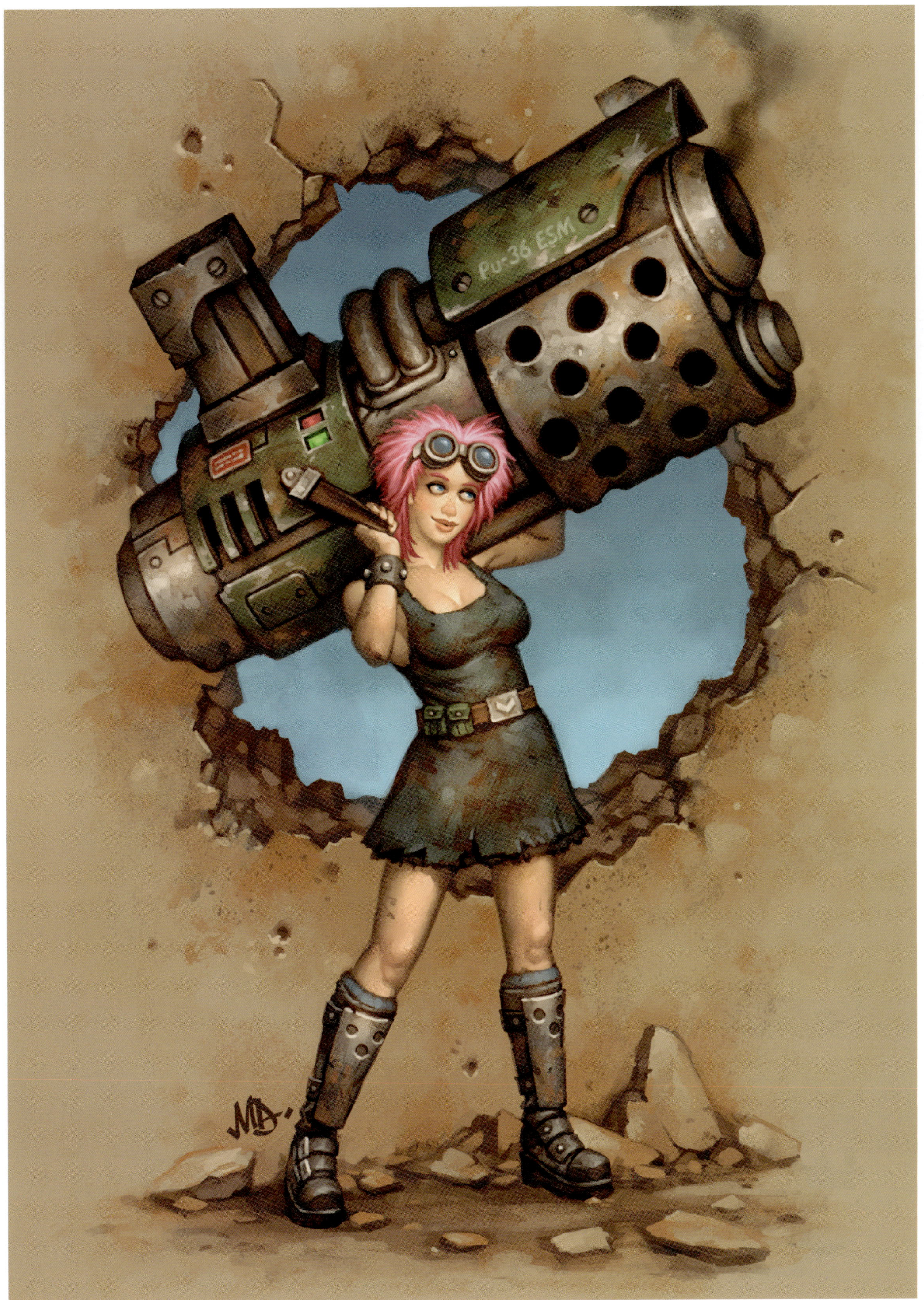

BFG!

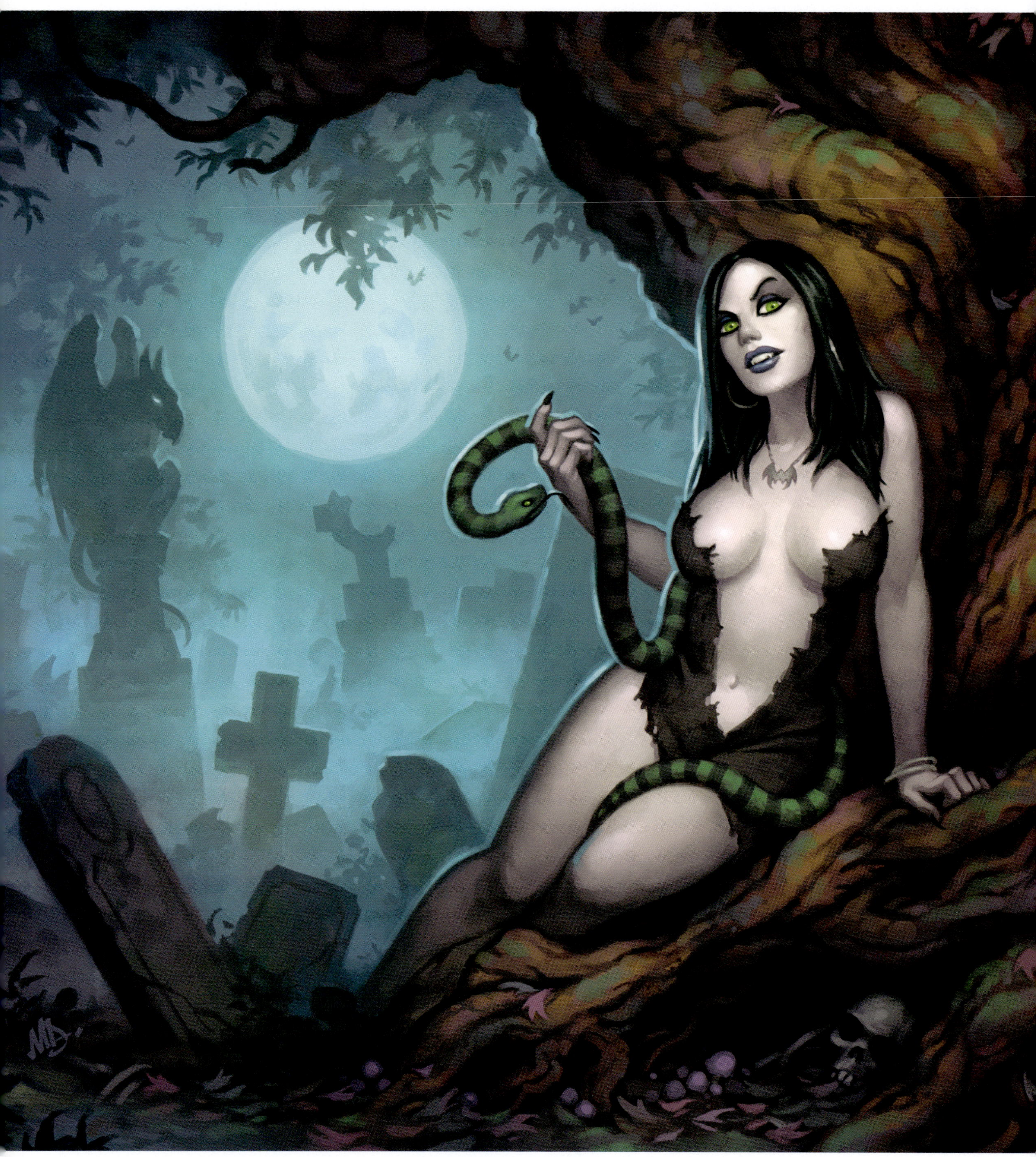

Grave Decision

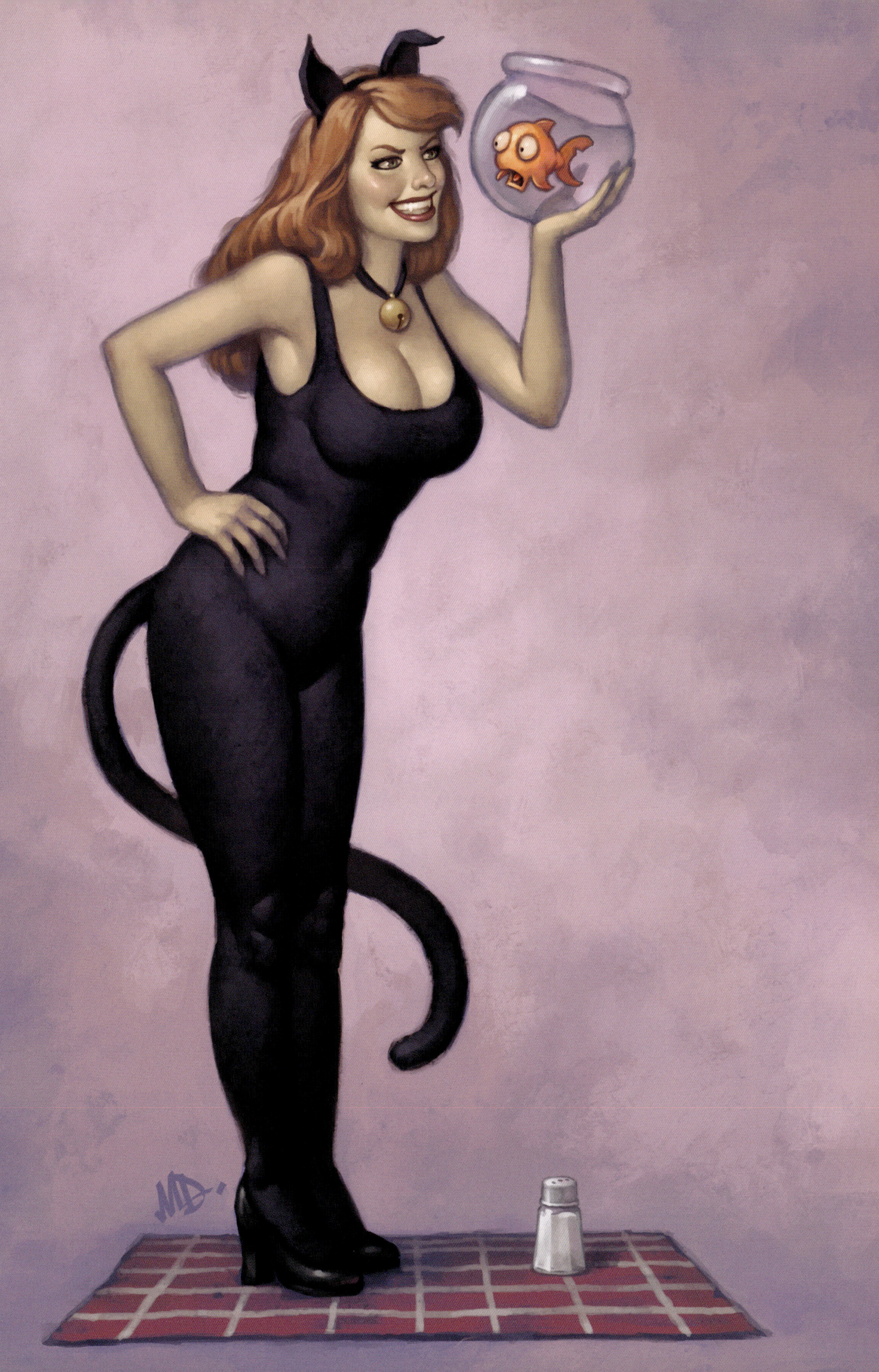

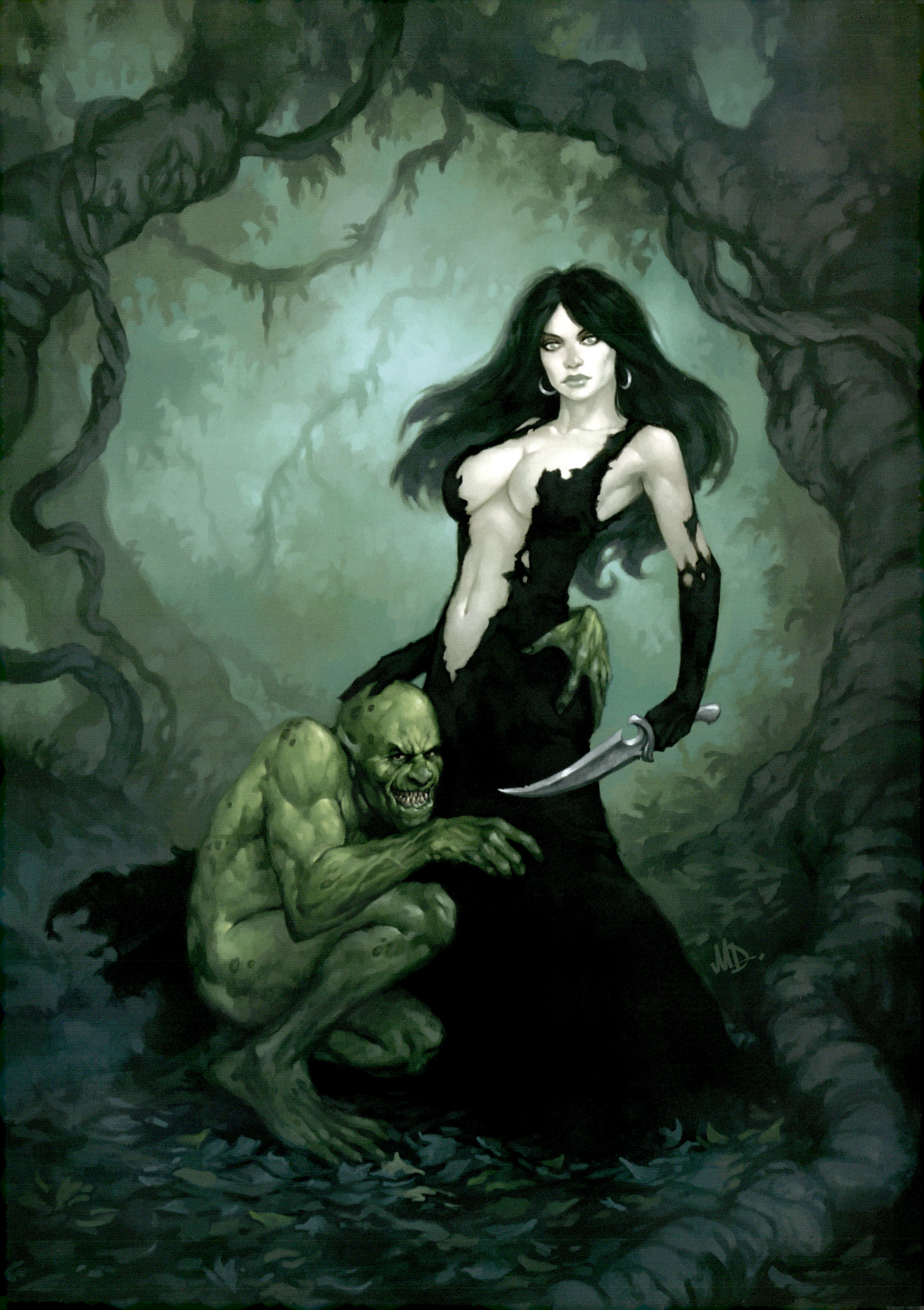

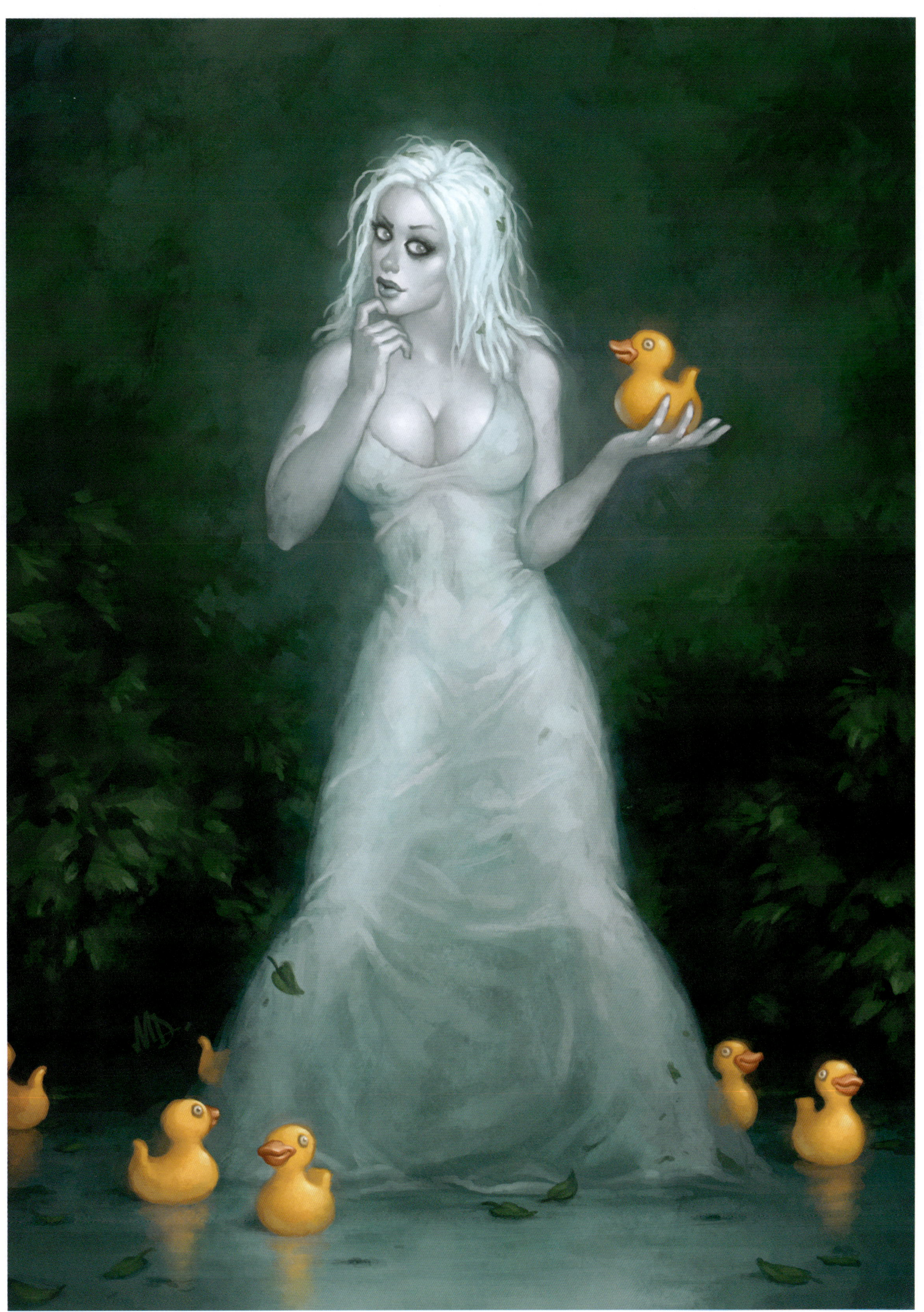

Visitors in the Drowning Pool

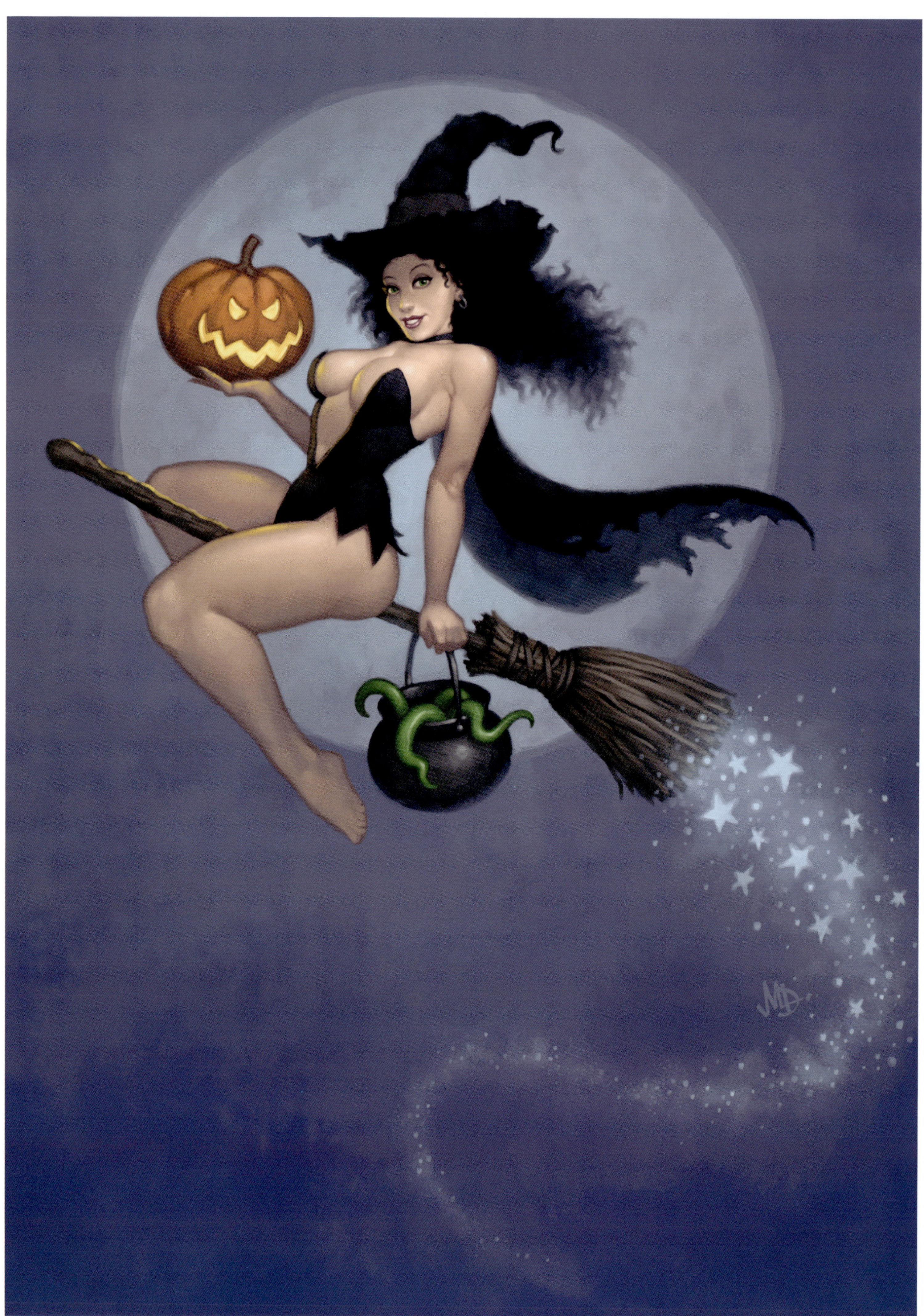

Va-Va-Va-Broom

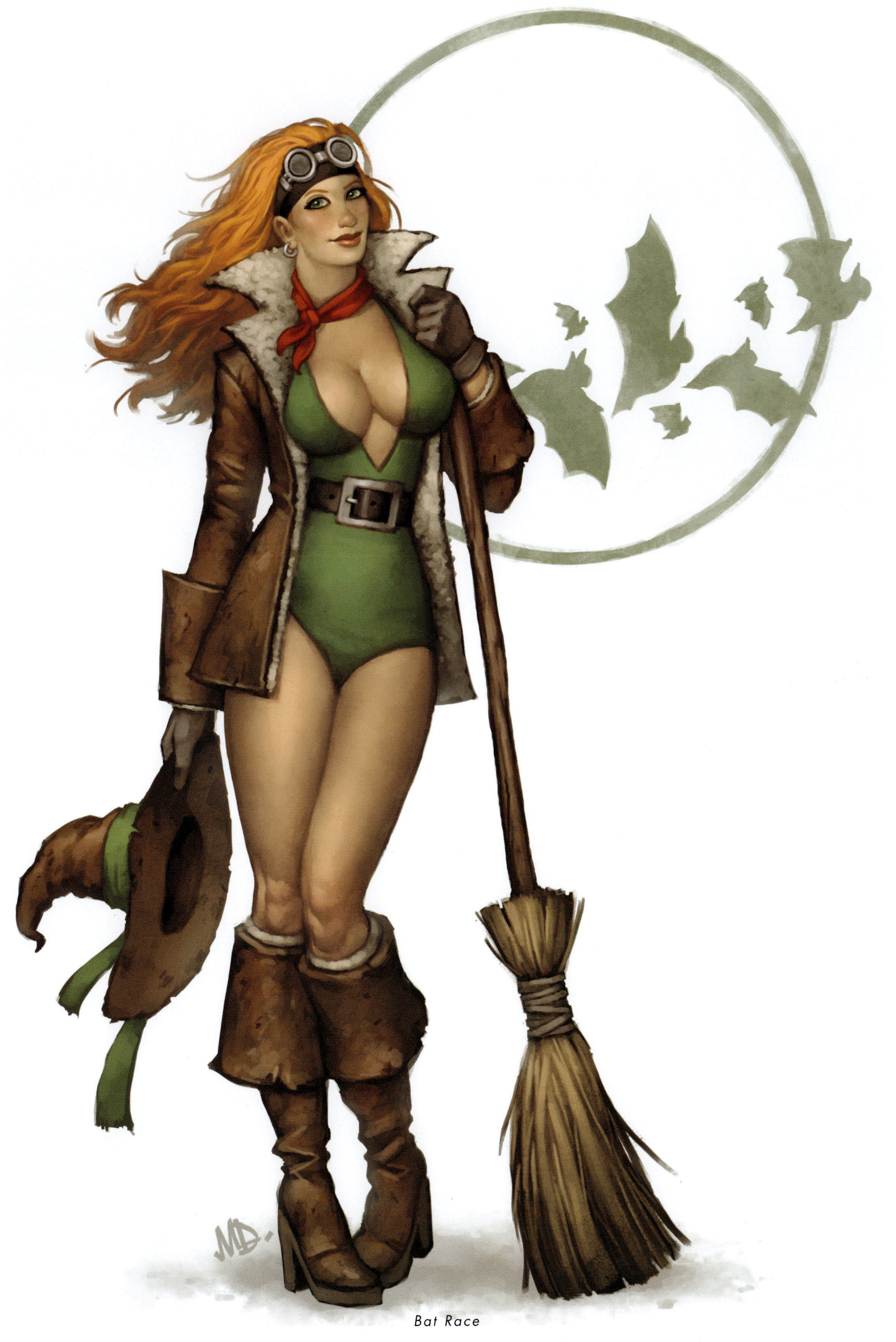

Bat Race

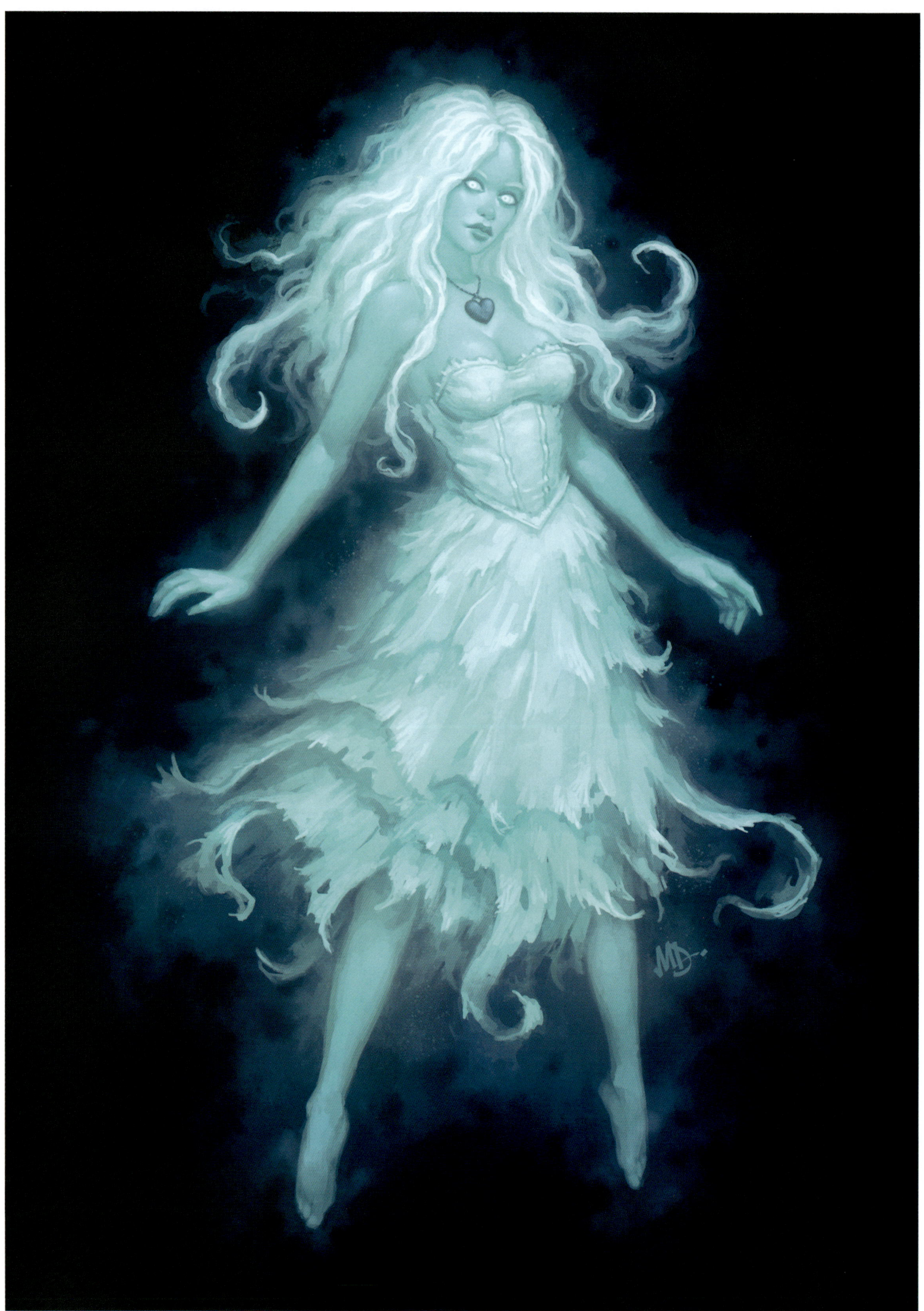

Ghost

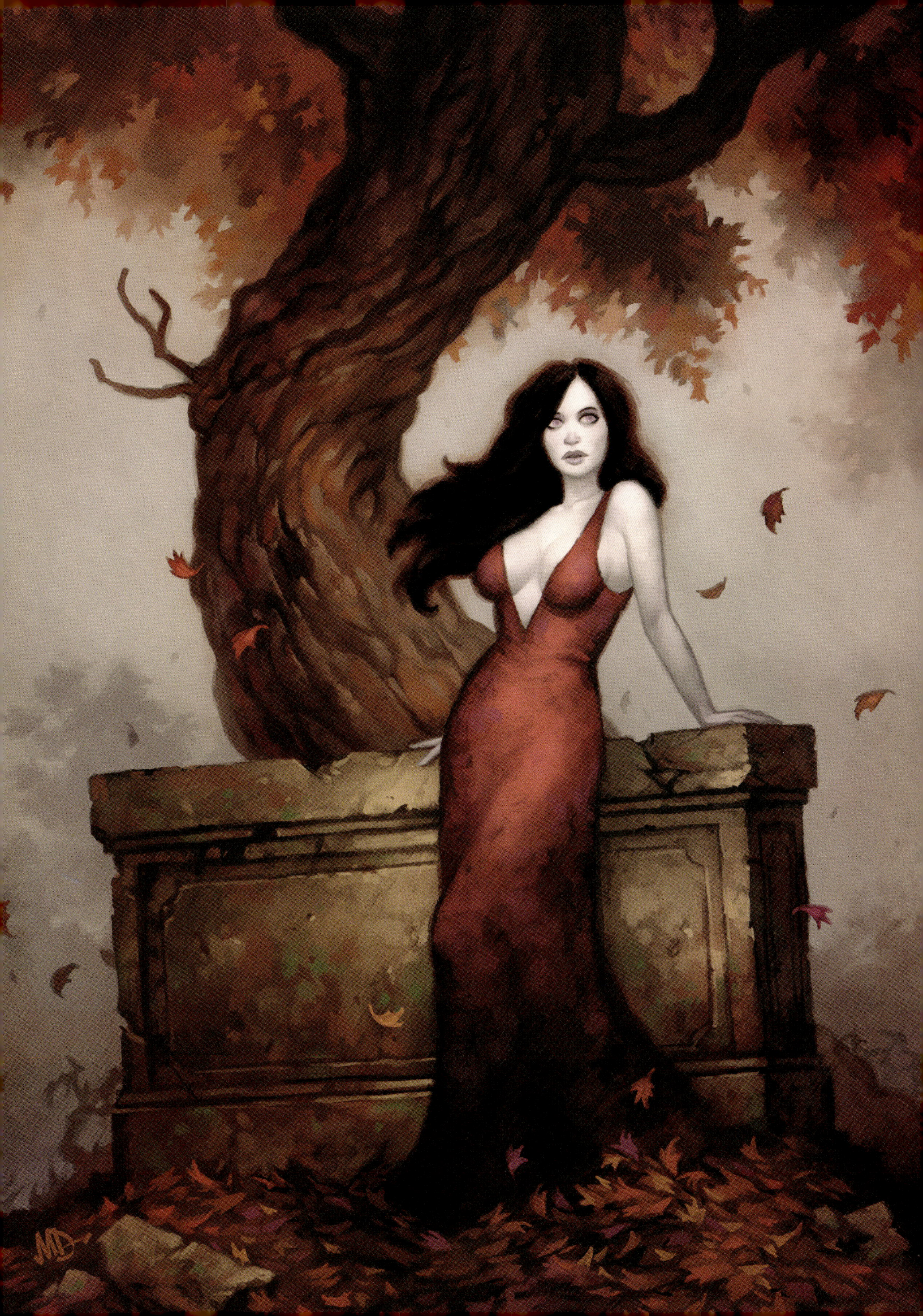

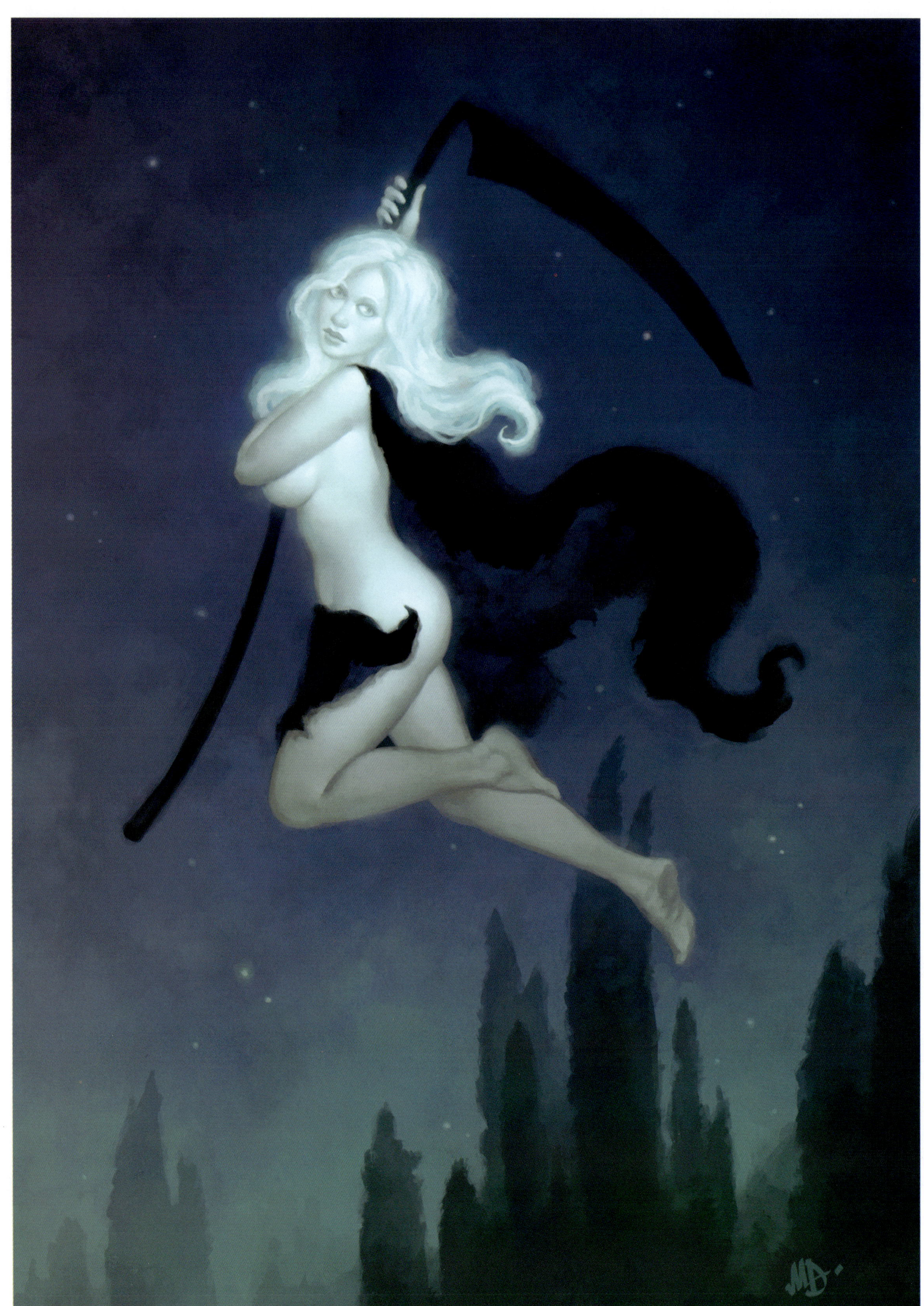

The Messenger

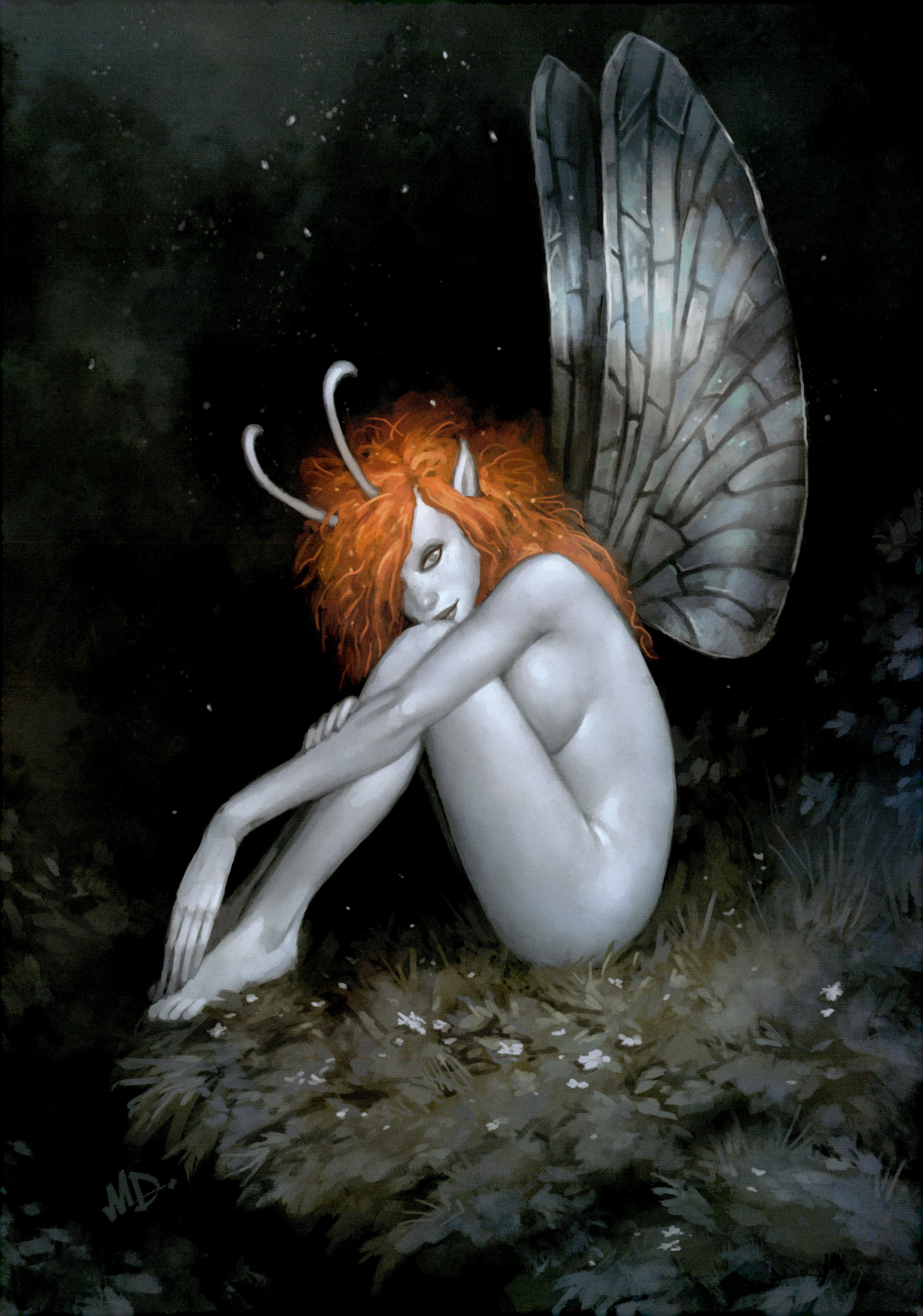

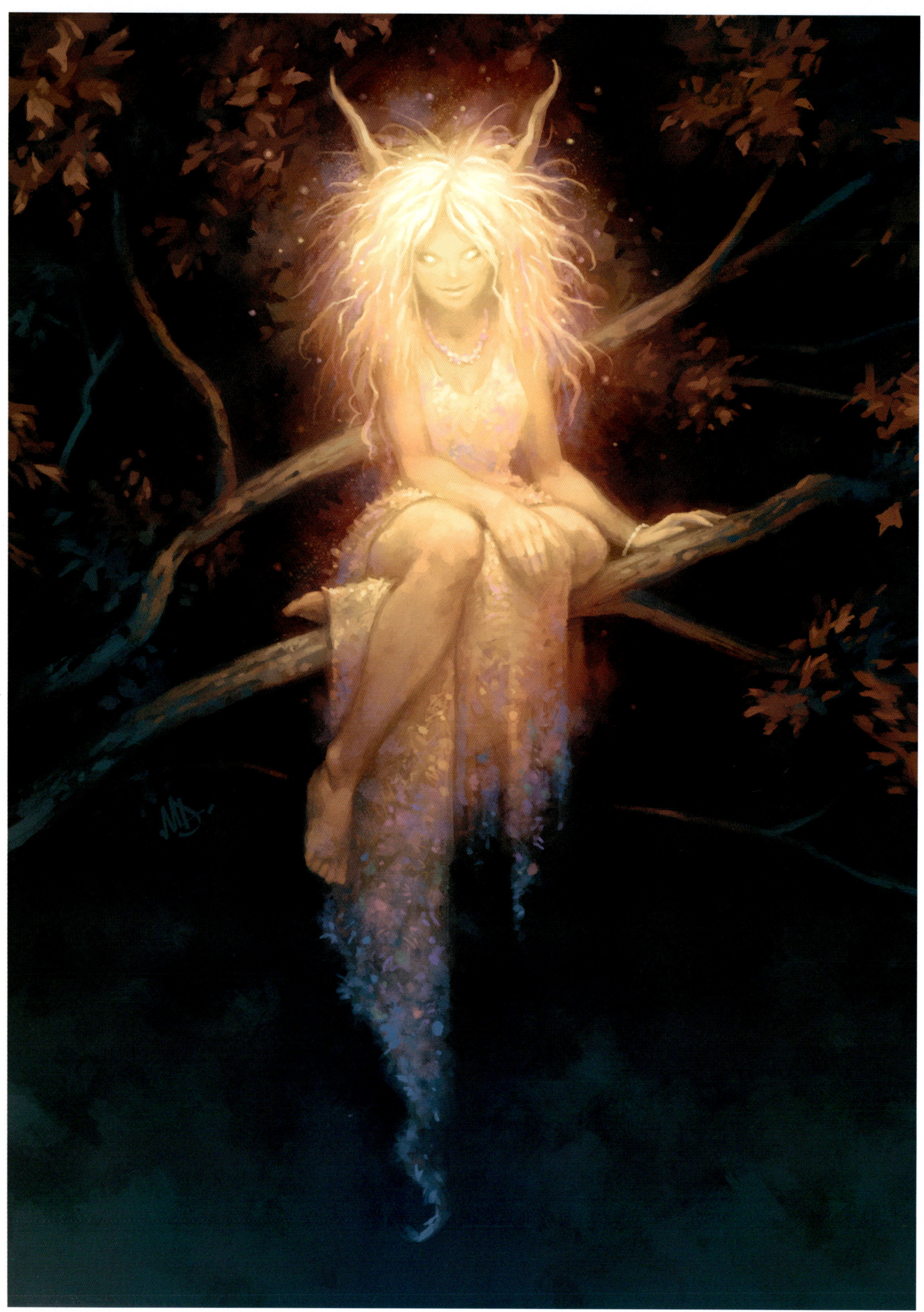

Titania

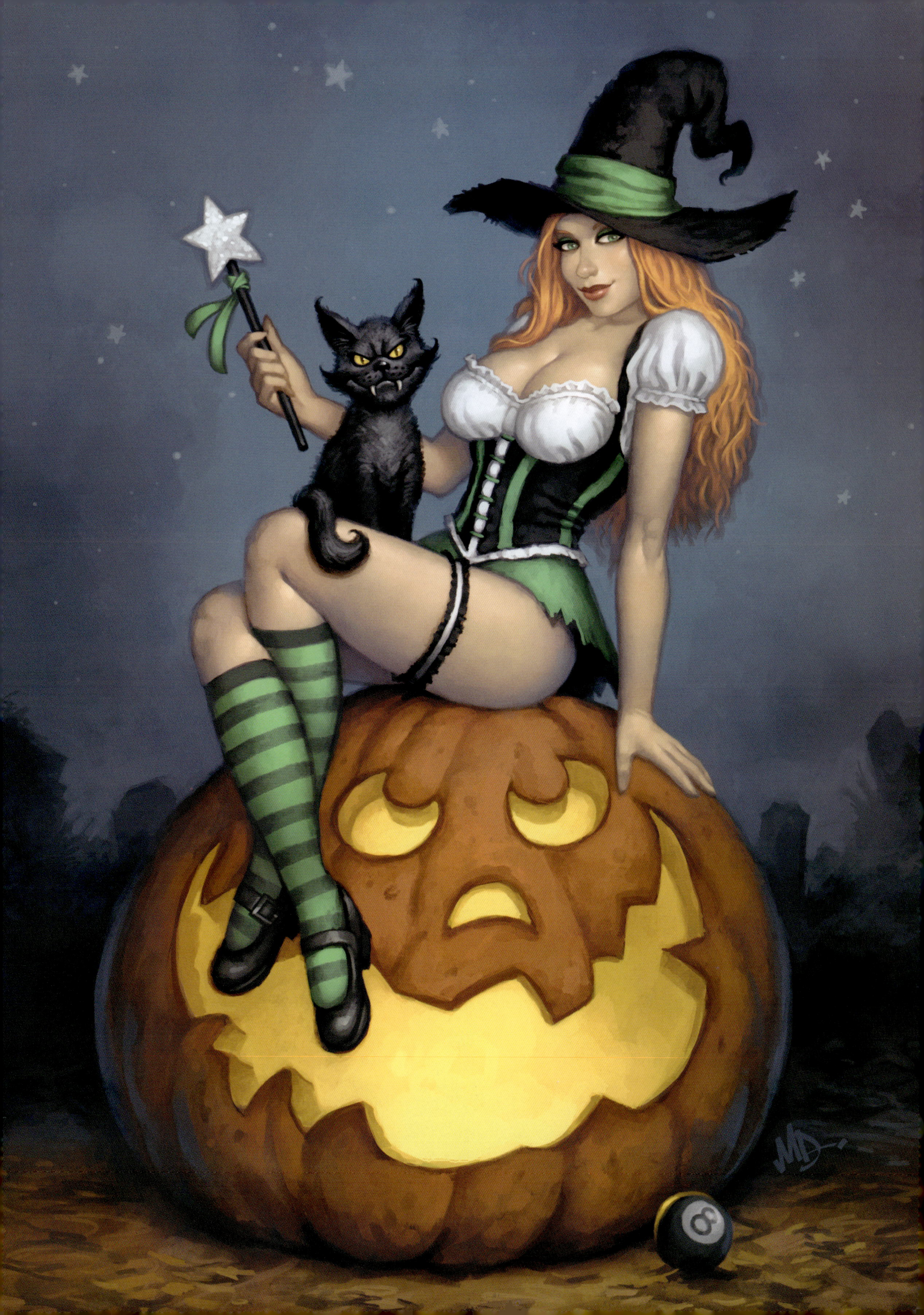

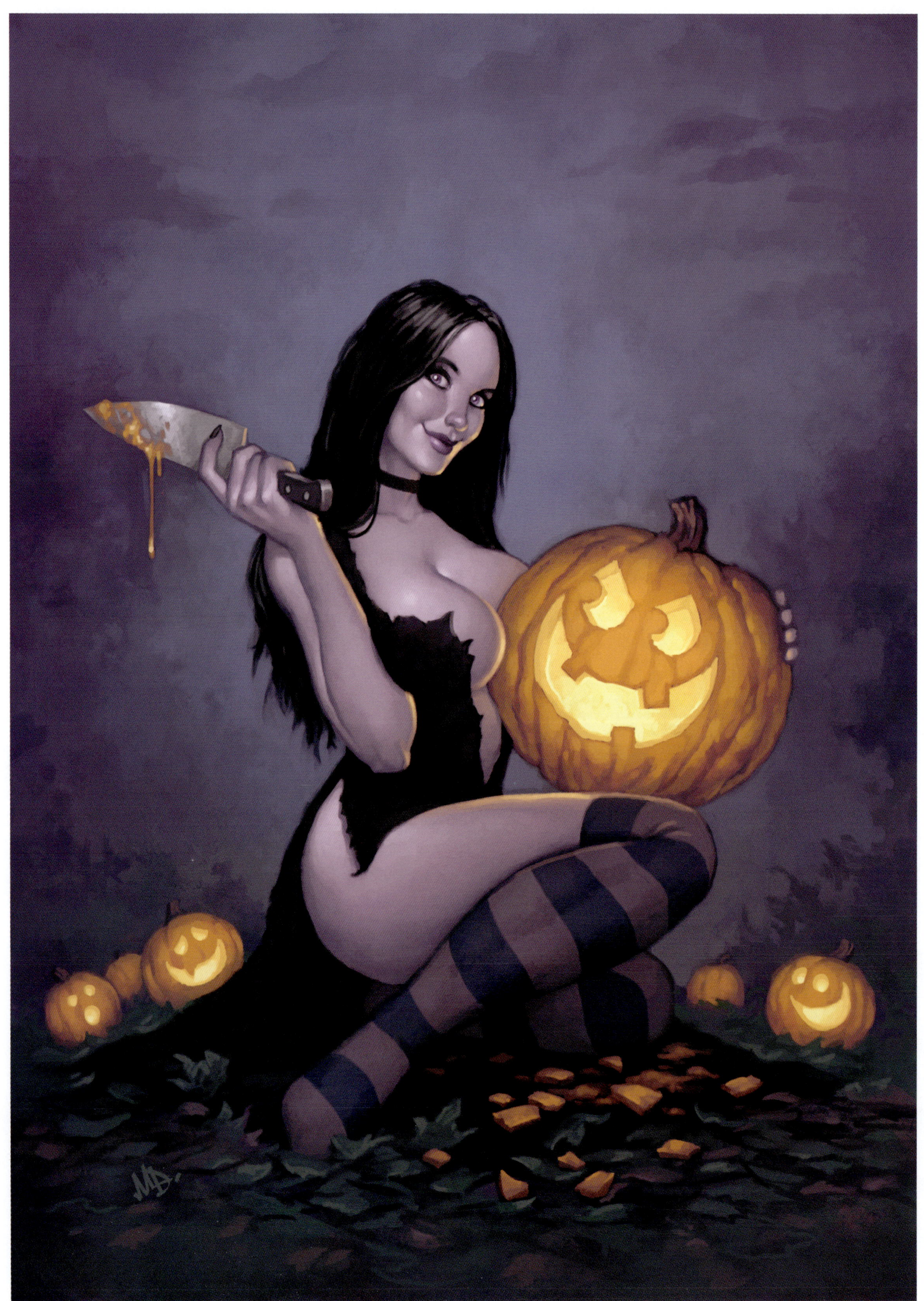

Trick or Treat

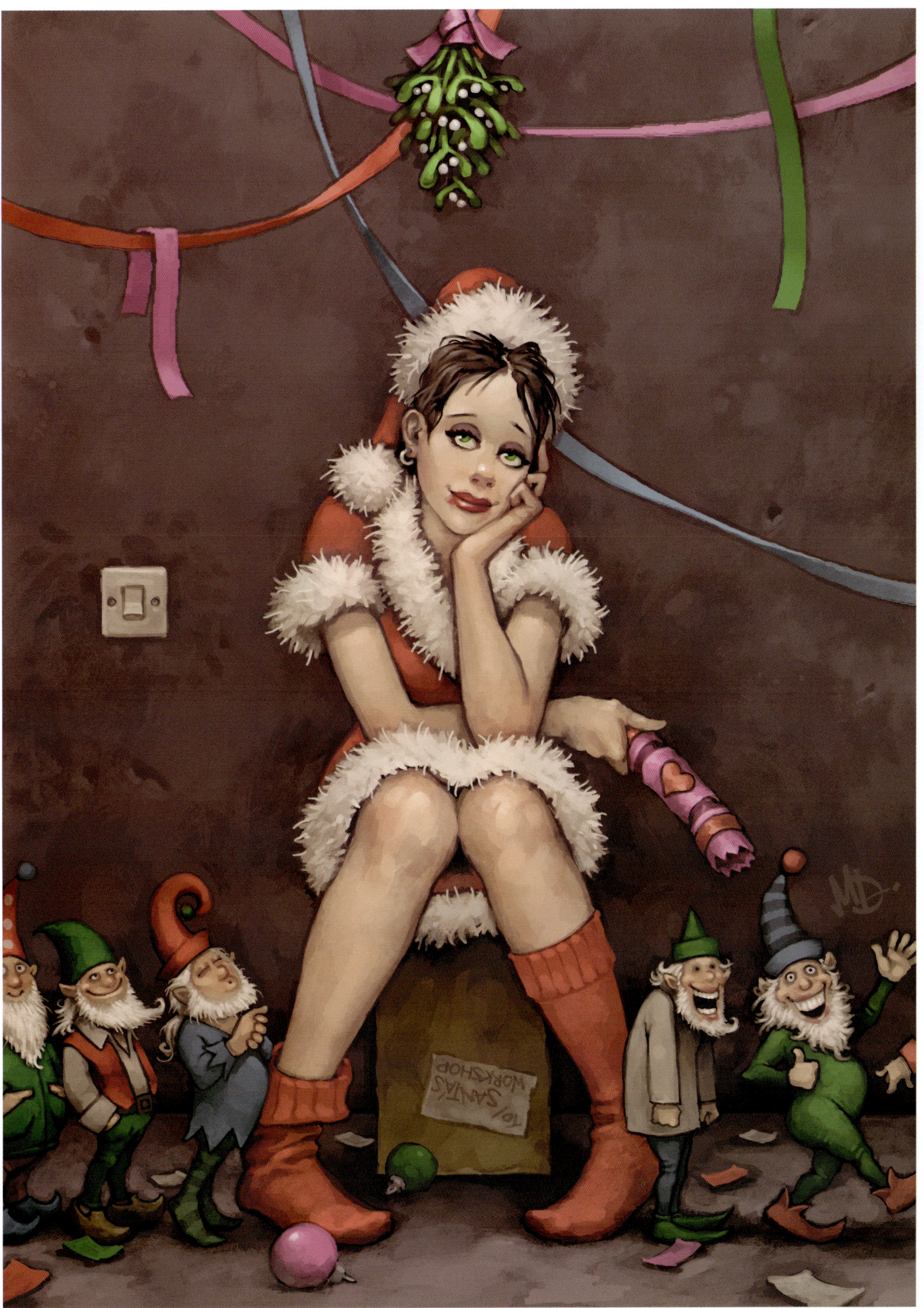

Happy Holidays

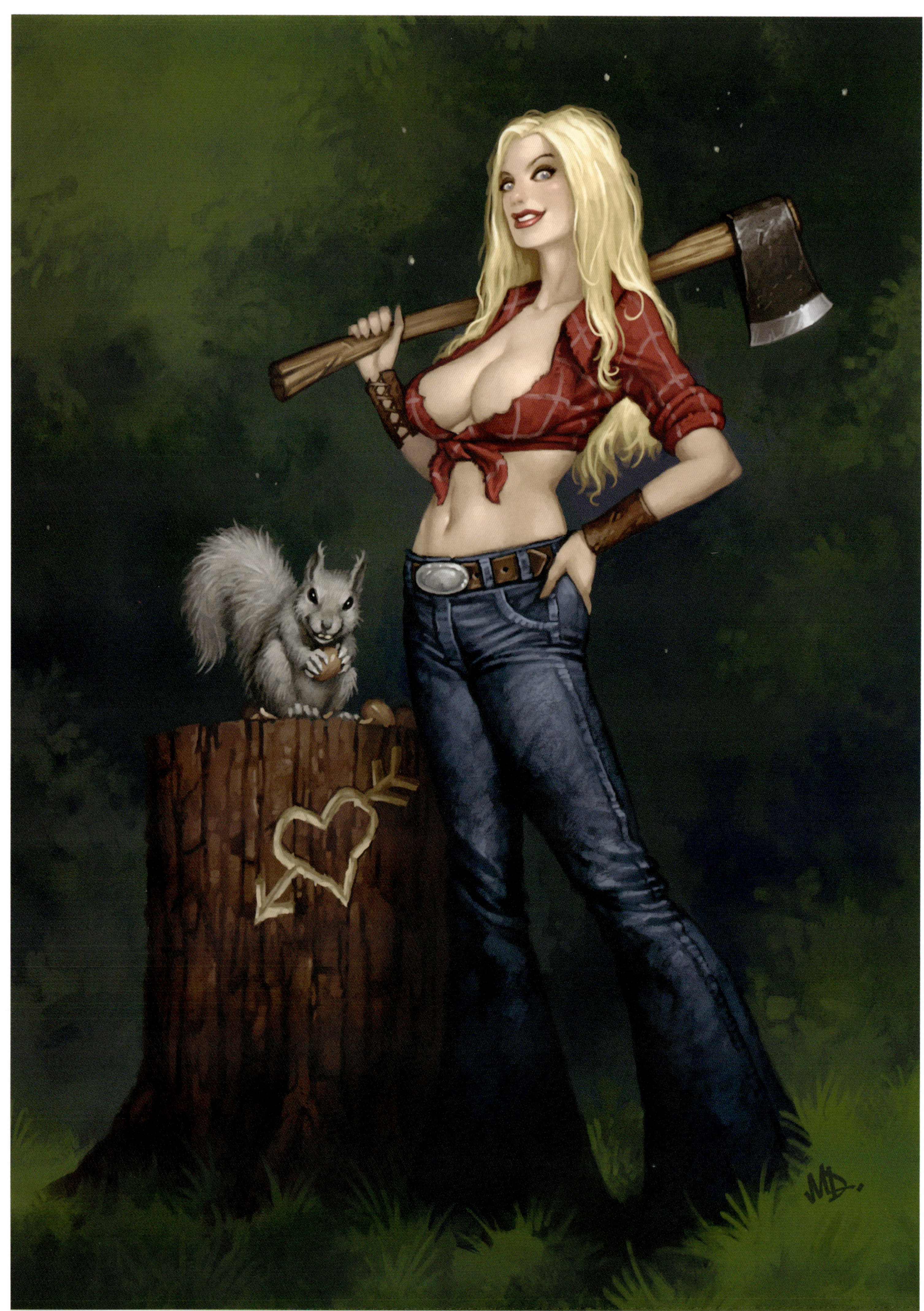

Lumberjill

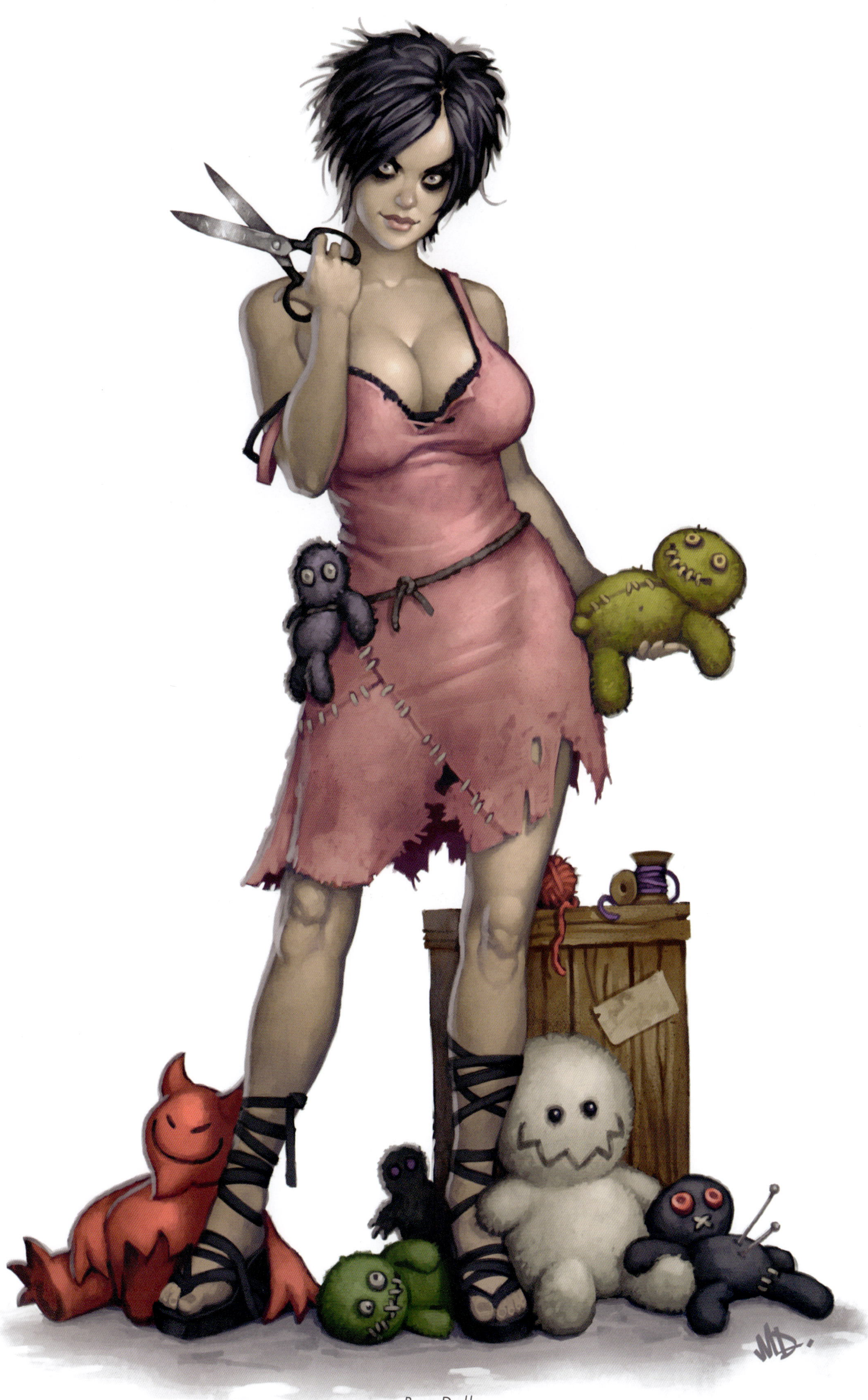

Rag Dolls

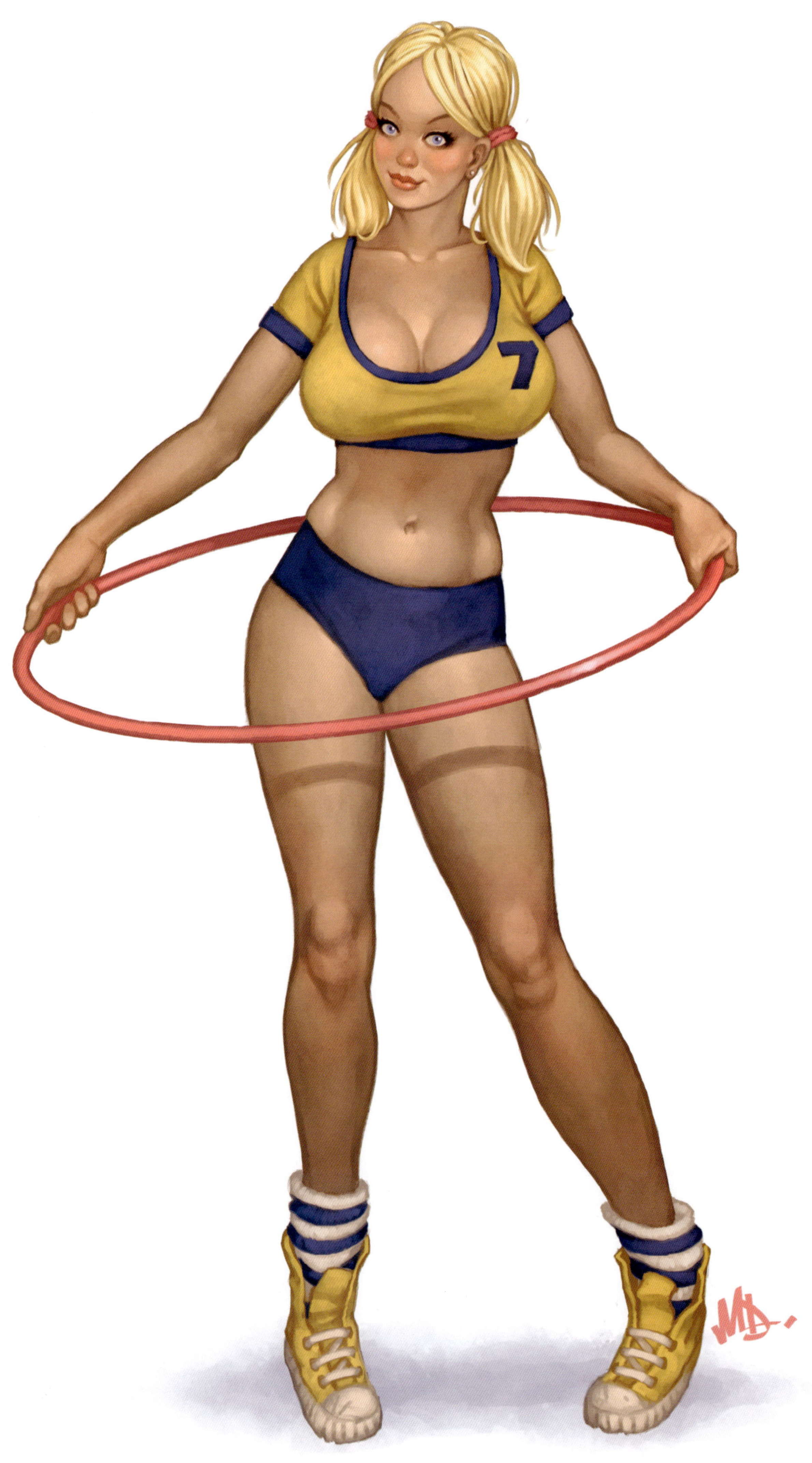

Hula Honey

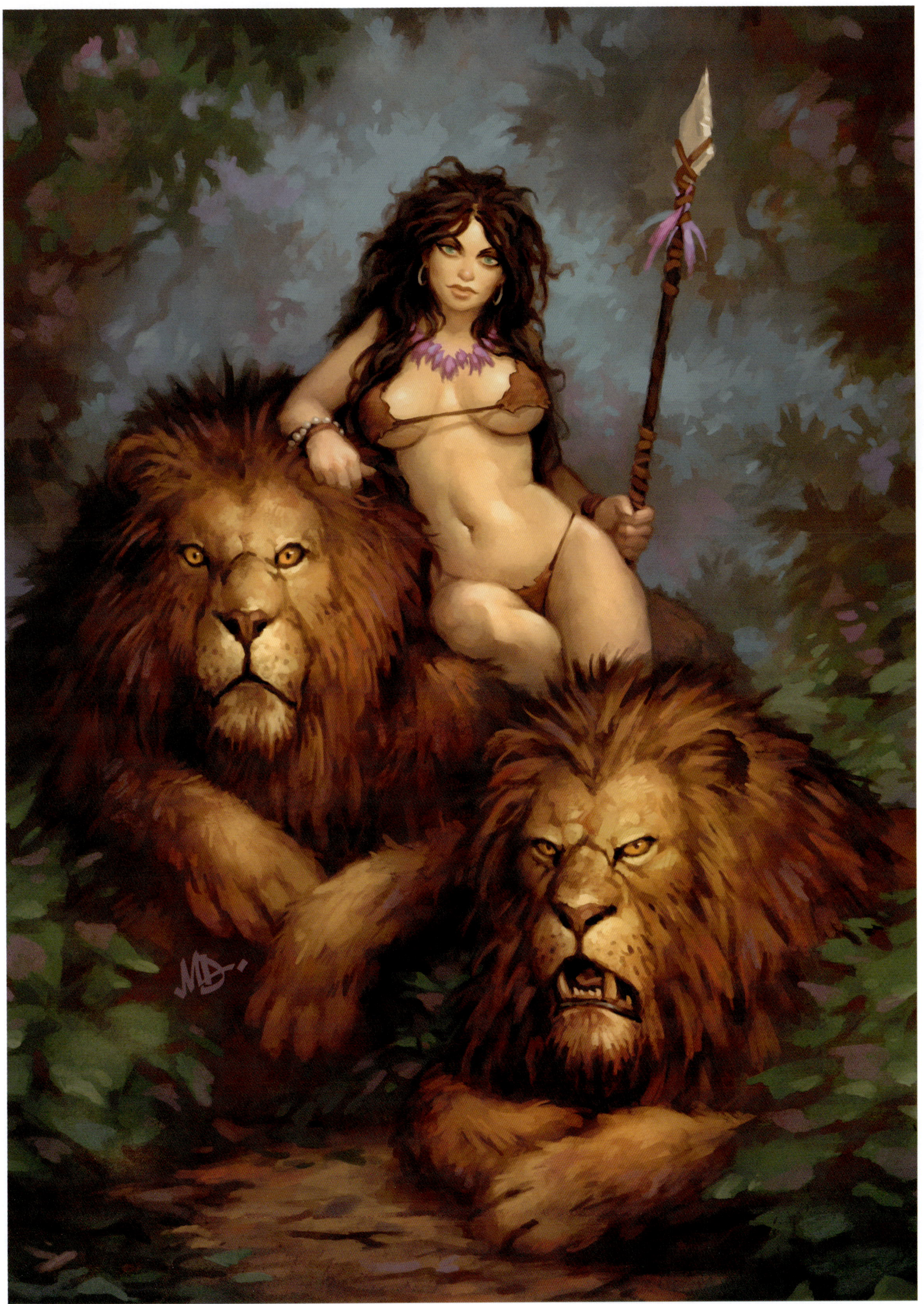

Mane Attraction

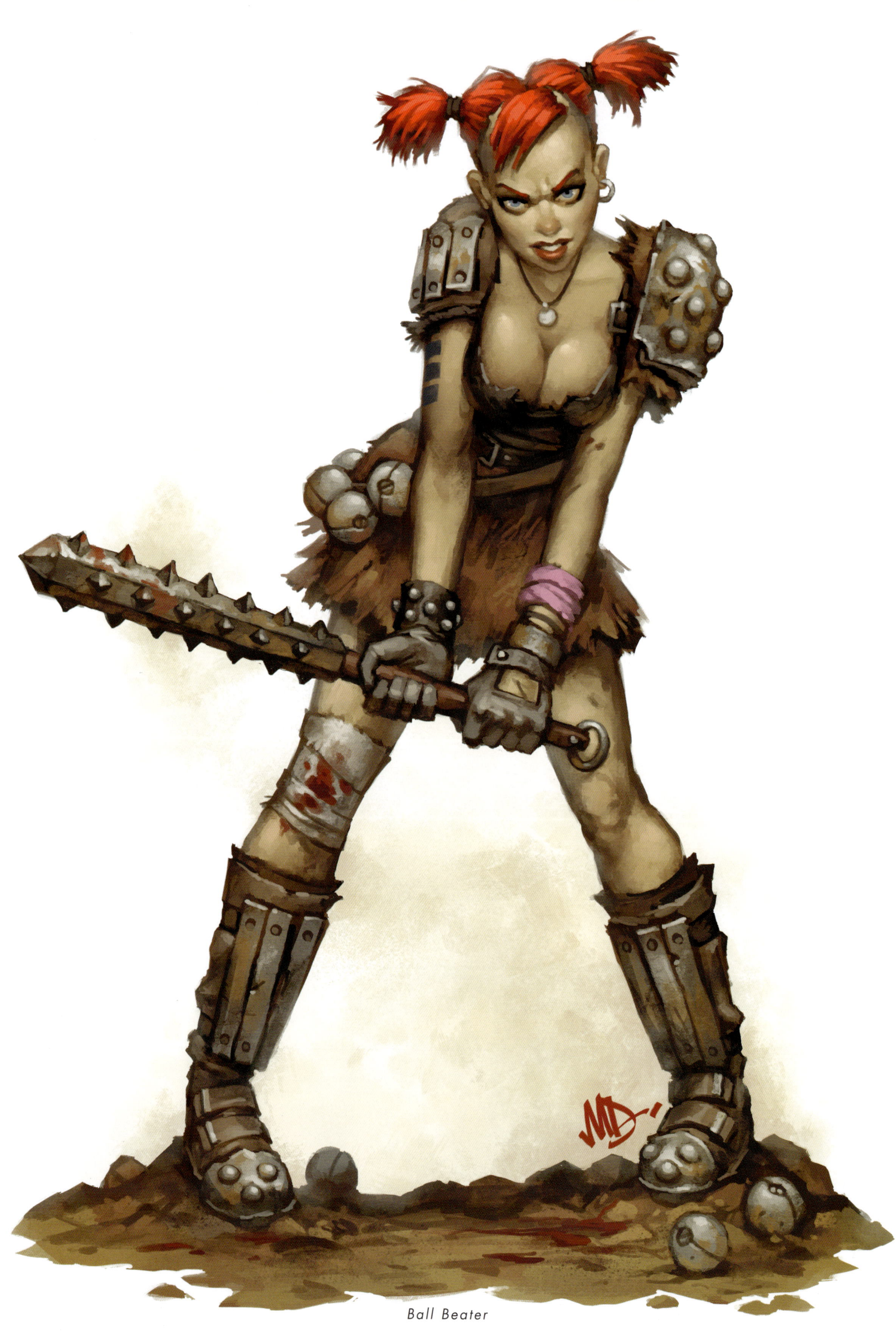

Ball Beater

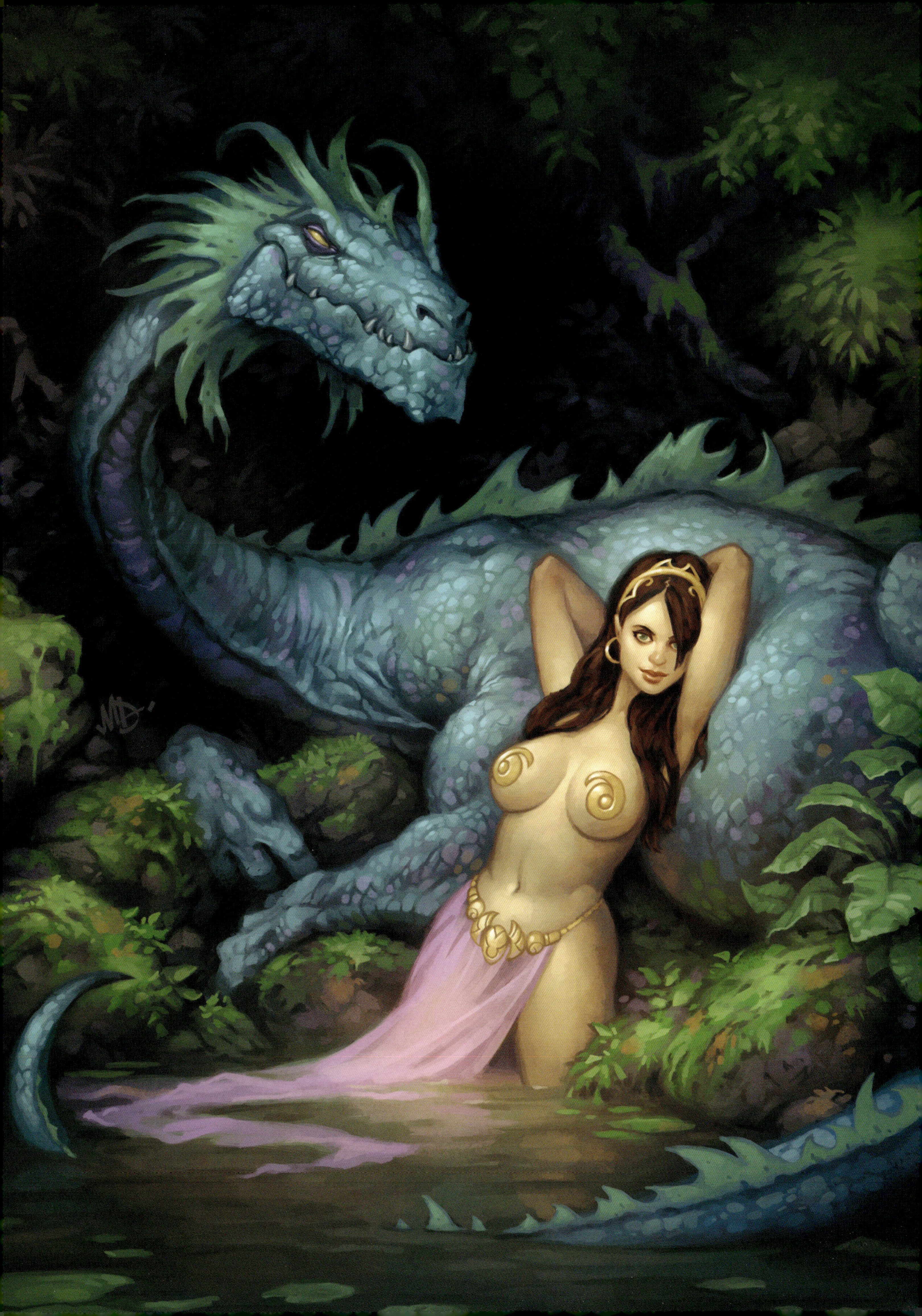

Artist's Step-By-Step:
Drinkerbell - from concept to completion

1) Sketch

Always begin your artwork by sketching out your idea. That may seem obvious but a great many folks seem to want to jump right in with color before taking the time to develop the concept or plan the image. The sketch is the foundation on which all your subsequent creative efforts will rest, so it's worth spending the time here to get things right. Ensure that the figure is correctly proportioned and well posed and that all the significant elements of the image are in place before calling the sketch done.

2) Value

Woah there, Leonardo - not time for color yet! The next step is to establish the values for your artwork by painting the sketch with grey tones. Values control the contrast, and therefore the focal areas, of the image in addition to defining form and separating shapes and planes. Placing the values independently of color allows for more deliberate control over these important elements.

3) Color

It's colorin' time! Develop a basic color palette on top of the value sketch. This is easily done using layers if working digitally, or with transparent washes if working with real paint. Digital paint is a particular advantage here as it allows for easy experimentation with different color schemes. Simple is usually best, so a limited palette of just two or three principal colors is a good place to start.

4) Render

The sketch is in place, values are laid in and the color palette is chosen - the finish line is in sight! All that remains is to build on what's already there. Render up the forms, adding light and shadow to give volume, taking care to differentiate between different materials and cleaning any rough edges. Avoid fine details for now as they make this process more laborious. Concentrate on the big shapes and working with the pattern of values established earlier.

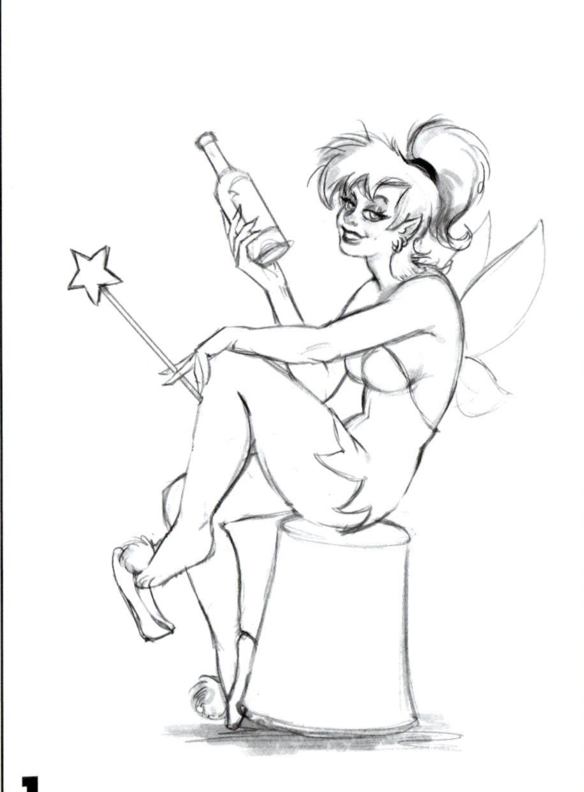

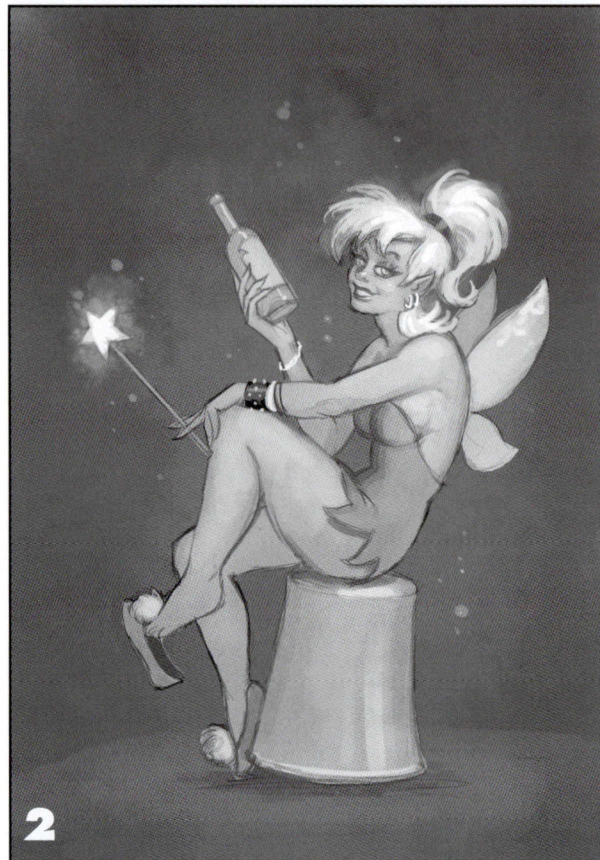

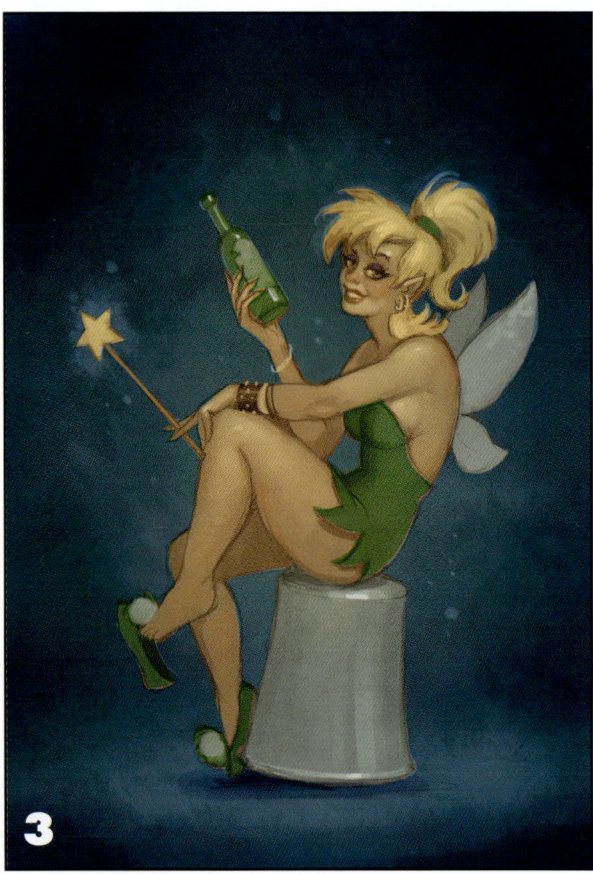

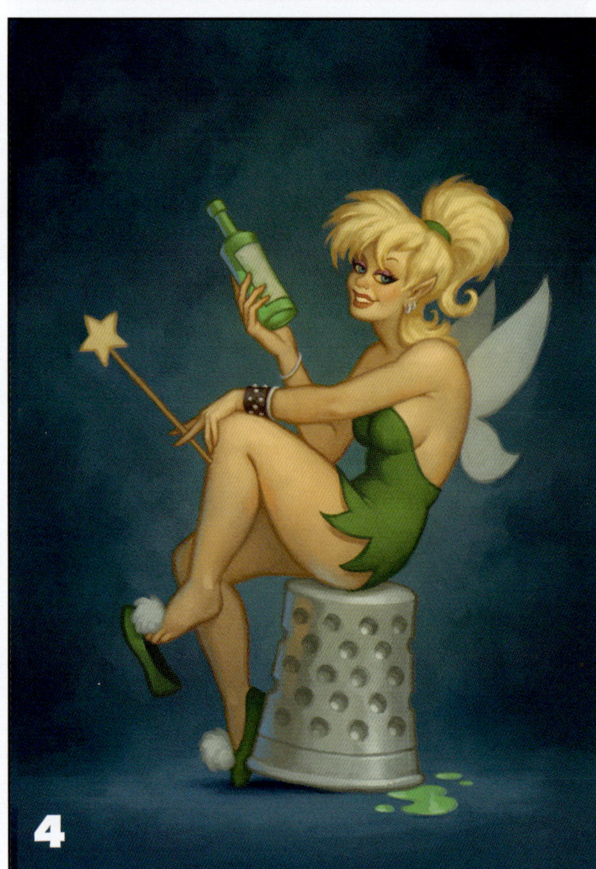

5) Finishing Touches

Once everything is neat and tidy, the picture just needs final details and a squirt of polish. Just how much is a matter of personal taste, though be careful not to get carried away and bury all that hard work under too many special effects and flourishes. Drinkerbell just needs a tattoo and a sprinkle of fairy dust and she's ready to hit the town..!

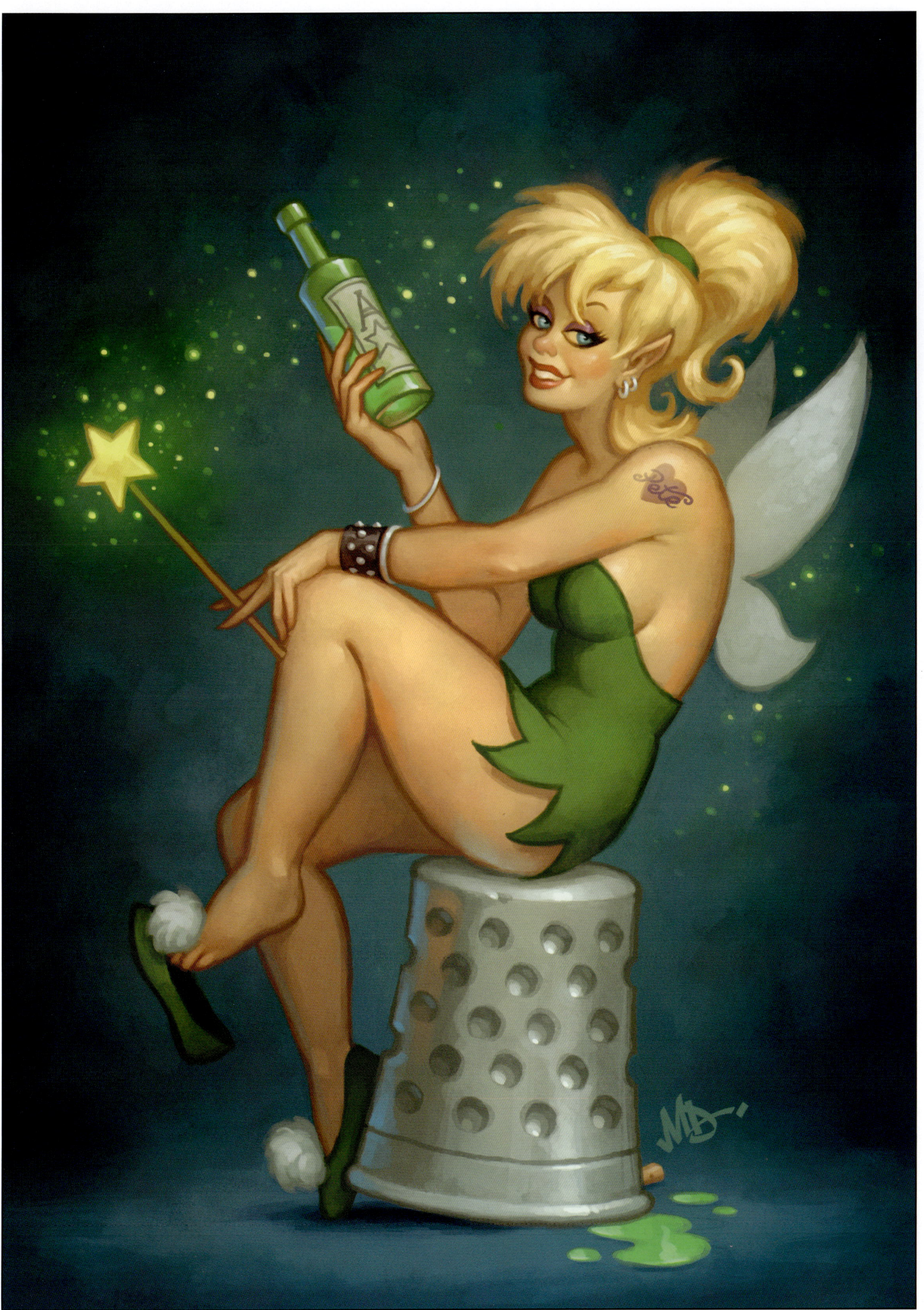

Drinkerbell

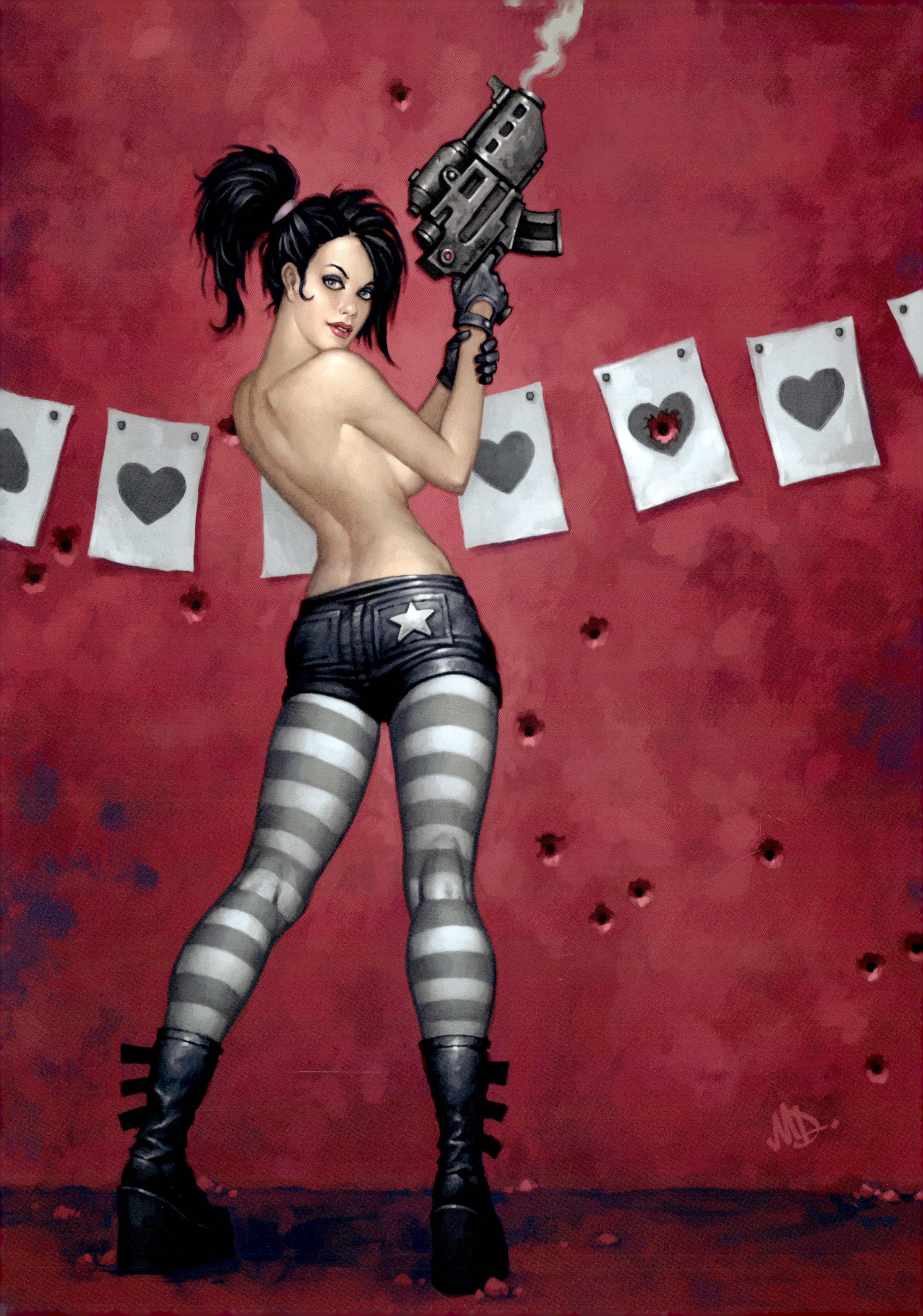